CW01401977

SELF-CATERING
AFLOAT

OTHER SELF-CATERING GUIDES PUBLISHED BY CHRISTOPHER HELM

Self-catering in France
Arthur and Barbara Eperon

Self-catering in Greece, Mainland and Islands
Florica Kyriacopoulos and Tim Salmon

Self-catering in Italy
Susan Grossman

Self-catering in Portugal
Carol Wright

Self-catering in Spain
Carole Stewart with Chris Stewart

SELF-CATERING

AFLOAT

<u>The</u> guide to wining and dining,
aboard and abroad

Bill Glenton

CHRISTOPHER HELM
London

© 1987 Bill Glenton
Line drawings by Mike Dodd
Maps by Peter Theodousiou
Christopher Helm (Publishers) Ltd, Imperial House,
21-25 North Street, Bromley, Kent BR1 1SD

British Library Cataloguing in Publication Data

Glenton, Bill
  Self-catering afloat.
  1. Cookery, Marine
  I. Title
  641.5'753   VC370

  ISBN 0-7470-1213-X

Typeset by Leaper and Gard Ltd, Bristol
Printed and bound in the Channel Islands by
The Guernsey Press Co. Ltd, Channel Islands

Contents

PART III SELF-CATERING AT SEA

1

Introduction

On any self-catering holiday it's that great sense of un-inhibited freedom that is such a big attraction: not being tied down by hotel meals or the other restrictions of a package hotel deal. If that is true about do-as-you-like stays ashore then it applies even more so for holidays afloat.

It is why increasingly thousands of people are becoming water gypsies — hiring motor craft on the many inland water-ways throughout the British Isles, across Europe and even as far away as America and Australia. There is also a smaller but equally fast growing trend towards taking seagoing sailing holidays, particularly of the 'flotilla' kind for newcomers to yachting.

For those taking to water for the first time it also means adapting to a more *al fresco* kind of catering or applying more ingenuity in cooking satisfying main meals afloat. In the cramped surroundings of a small boat with just a tiny galley with its two- or three-ring mini-stove you have to concentrate your methods as well as your mind.

The purpose of this first ever guide to catering afloat for hire craft users is to help steer readers to an easier, simpler way of enjoying their holiday by taking away many of the problems and much of the sweat of preparing and cooking suitable and satisfying meals. It also covers how to go about and get the best out of shopping in foreign lands as well as suggesting useful landmarks when eating out in local restaur-ants or when picnicking.

At the same time plenty of useful information is provided about the kinds of boat holidays available; types of craft and how they are equipped; the most attractive areas for both inland and seagoing cruising; plus a host of other handy advice on helpful matters from clothing and medical aids to the addresses of specialist hire firms.

What will clearly emerge from this guide is how much greater the choice of these water-borne vacations is than most people believe. The areas alone are considerable. They stretch from the British Isles north all the way to Scandinavia and Finland, south through France to the Mediterranean and as far east as Greece and Turkey. And these areas do not include the vast choice available in the United States.

Indeed, the potential in the British Isles is far greater than you might imagine. The current network of rivers, canals and lochs on which hire craft operate covers thousands of miles — all the way from southern England and East Anglia through the Midlands to central and North Wales, up to the North of England and as far as the Highlands of Scotland — and this network is increasing slowly all the time. Across the Irish Sea there are hundreds of miles of good waterways in both Ulster and the Republic.

It would take annual holidays for a decade to take advantage of the massive network in France, the most popular area for cruising Britons abroad. But Holland with its big selection is also becoming a busy floating playground and a sizeable number have begun adventuring along the abundant choice of rivers and lakes in Denmark, Sweden, Norway and Finland.

More remarkable, perhaps, is the fairly recent growth in people, often newcomers or just used to dinghy sailing, who have decided boldly to launch themselves on less placid waters by joining the new-style 'flotilla' yachts operating in the Adriatic, eastern Mediterranean and Aegean. Scores of these craft, with both sails and engine, are now available through a dozen specialist companies offering inclusive fly-cruise deals. Catering aboard them calls for particular advice — which this guide provides.

What *Self-catering Afloat* also does is to try and help you choose the right type of craft from the very big choice available, both inland and seagoing, that will best suit your needs, skills and size of party, taking into account their catering possibilities.

You can hire a cosy little boat for two or three or anything up to a cruiser with 10 or 12 berths. Sleek motor cruisers ranging up to 'gin palace' size might have much swashbuckling appeal but Mum with three lively children to look after could find it easier and safer catering for them in one of the many 'narrow boats' with their longer, more convenient layout. Since all craft have to keep to a slow speed on most waterways you lose nothing from putting comfort before show. But there are so many different types and sizes almost everyone's tastes and basic needs are catered for.

As thousands have already found there is no previous experience needed in handling inland waterway craft, especially if you can drive a car — just common sense and the useful list of instructions provided by the hire company. A test run is always made under supervision before you set out. Firms offering flotilla holidays usually demand that one person has previous yacht-handling experience or, at the least, dinghy sailing knowledge. They will arrange short training courses as well.

At each appropriate cruising area section in the guide details of the holiday companies operating in them is given as well as the name and address of the national tourist office, which can usually provide extra printed information about the region and other useful data. Most travel agents provide the cruising firms' brochures, although for some you may have to write direct to the company. The length of holidays can range from three to four days in Britain to one or two weeks both in the UK and abroad. For anyone seeking a holiday that combines cruising with a stay ashore, perhaps to satisfy a family argument or because they just want to sample a hire craft, they can find a good choice of self-catering land and sea deals.

Much of the advice given in these pages has been obtained at first-hand by the author over many years of cruising in the British Isles and overseas. When necessary, he has obtained the expert knowledge of others to fill any gaps, especially regarding recipes and other good catering tips. Generally, this guide is intended to help the newcomer to self-catering afloat but it is hoped that it will also extend the waterborne horizons of the many who are already committed water gypsies.

USING THIS BOOK

The guide falls into two main categories: self-catering on inland waterways and catering in seagoing craft. There are chapters describing the range of hire boats available; details of typical layouts; areas in which the types of craft are found; and a variety of useful information needed to make each type of holiday more enjoyable, easier and safer.

Since both categories cover such a wide-spanning international scene, each has been divided into sub-sections according to country or sea. For convenience, each of the sub-sections contains all the detailed information relevant to that area such as local shopping, eating out and catering advice. With the exception of most of the Scandinavian countries, where only one list of translated useful words and phrases is given (Swedish is a fairly common tongue), helpful interpretations of names of foodstuffs and menu items are provided with each area.

Although the guide concentrates on the British Isles and the Continent, a small section is devoted to possibilities for enjoying similar cruising in such areas as the USA and Australia.

I have not attempted to give any holiday prices since these are always subject to alteration, as are some of the inclusive arrangements and cruise itineraries. New operators will arrive on this active scene and some of those listed might disappear, so it is essential to check directly with operators or through travel agents before attempting to book.

PART I

INLAND WATERWAYS: THE BASICS

2
The Pleasures of Cruising

Cruising rivers, canals or lakes has been likened to having a caravan on water. To some extent this is true since there is a similar compactness of space and fittings and you do share the same spirit of independence. Anyone who has tried catering in a caravan with its limited cooking and storage facilities will also be better able to handle the tasks in a cramped boat.

But the prospect of handling a boat and its equipment often seems more daunting — even for those who can expertly tow a large, swaying caravan down lanes narrower than most waterways. Perhaps it is the uncertainty engendered when swopping firm dry land for water or it could even be a fear associated with the mystique that seems to surround anything nautical.

The simple fact, however, is that operating a typical waterway craft is normally a darn sight easier than driving a car — certainly one pulling a caravan in a gusting wind. Compare the accident rate between highways and waterways and there is no doubt which is far, far safer. One rarely hears of serious accidents on inland waterways, and considering that the top speed of most of their craft is limited to around seven knots, then this is not surprising. And only on broad lakes are you likely to run any risk of rough weather.

No one with any Toad of Toad Hall ambitions to go full belt should even consider this type of cruising. Indeed, it is the easy-going pace of this kind of holiday — hardly much faster than someone strolling along the towpath — combined with your closeness to so much scenic nature, that is its great charm. You would land yourself straight into trouble if you did not show full consideration for other waterway users. Not slowing down when passing moored craft so as to avoid making an upsetting wash, and not observing the few 'Rules of the Road', such as the proper places to give way to oncoming boats and keeping to your correct side, are misdemeanours you should avoid at all costs.

But there are very few other inhibitions in what is probably the most relaxed form of touring offered by any kind of holiday transport, apart from the physical limitations imposed by the waterway and any locks on it. Even going anywhere at all loses much of its appeal as you slowly become absorbed within the countryside and its wildlife all around. It can prove a mistake when planning your trip to aim for constant travel between places. You will be surprised by just how many distractions there are that keep you tied up for hours — by day as well as by night.

Although you are cruising along waterways that have been navigated for centuries you are still very much on a voyage of discovery. The views of even familiar places can look totally different seen from a river or canal. You often go where the roads cannot lead you — sometimes where walking is impossible such as marshes packed with bird life. And sailing through towns and cities gives you an intriguing behind-the-scenes view of life.

All the time, of course, you are carrying your holiday home with you like some giant water snail. But what makes a cruiser better than a caravan is that you can still enjoy and make use of the comforts and amenities of your floating home while you are underway. On quiet waters someone can be preparing a meal for the family or friends to enjoy immediately you tie up. None of that 'hurry up, I want to get moving' protest either when you need to get somewhere else.

There is also rather more freedom of choice when you are looking for a place to berth for lunch or a night's sleep; no desperate hunt for a caravan site with a spare space. Apart from obviously narrow parts where you might prevent another craft passing, most waterways offer plenty of spots to tie up without risk and there are also many specially created 'boat parks' available for a small charge. There is no reason why your personal refuelling point need not be some ancient Danish inn, a Dutch canalside bar, Swedish or Norwegian café or even a Finnish lakeside fish restaurant. Can there be a more pleasant or convenient way of going for a drink than mooring right alongside some British pub or French *estaminet*? No breathalysers are required for boat skippers.

What is so enjoyable about waterway holidays these days is the really rich choice of countries and totally different scenes in which to enjoy them. As this guide clearly shows in later chapters, it is comparatively simple to book cruises, often inclusive with ferry or air transport, over a good part of the Continent. British-based travel firms arrange most of these deals and no matter which country you decide upon there is a fairly common denominator where hire craft and their operation are concerned. If you have been cruising in Britain you will certainly be able to handle boats elsewhere and vice versa. There is no need to worry over which side of the 'road' to use or how to cope with left-hand drive. The catering equipment aboard and methods of cooking are also virtually the same wherever you cruise.

A big attraction for many Britons who do cruise on the Continent is the great choice of less crowded, often broader, waters than the mainly narrow rivers and canals of Britain, although there are some pretty substantial Scottish lochs and a number of broad waterways in both parts of Ireland. Some of the French rivers and Scandinavian lakes are quite wide although, generally, very safe to navigate. If it is really open water you are seeking then there are a few areas such as the west coast of Sweden, southern Norway and the outer Clyde where you can cruise between coastal islands or in sea lochs.

Wherever you go cruising there is no need to believe it is unsuitable for you because of age, family or social reasons. There are many boats on hire than can be perfectly well handled by 'Golden Oldies' or by a single person. Most are fine for parents with children and in my long experience the youngsters make fine crew members and are perfectly safe. There is also a *camaraderie* among most boat hirers that makes inland waterway holidays as democratic a pleasure as you will find anywhere.

YOUR BOAT

There it lies, bobbing gently up and down alongside the jetty. It looks watertight but there could be a sinking feeling in the pit of your stomach. It certainly did not look as small as that in the brochure! But even tinier craft have crossed the Atlantic and ones not much bigger have sailed around the world. And you are only going to spend a week or two in her.

Your fears may increase as you bump your head entering the saloon. Fortunately the raised cabin roof allows you to stand upright inside it. But there is a groan from cook as she gets her first sight of the minute galley. 'It's going to be sandwiches from now on', she insists. As events transpire she finds herself turning out some tasty hot dishes.

The children remain excited but wonder how they are going to sleep in that cabin squeezed into the curving bows with the deckhead just inches from their faces. Your own

Typical 2–4 berth motor cruiser, very suitable for novices.
Length 26ft.; beam 9ft. 6ins; headroom 6ft.

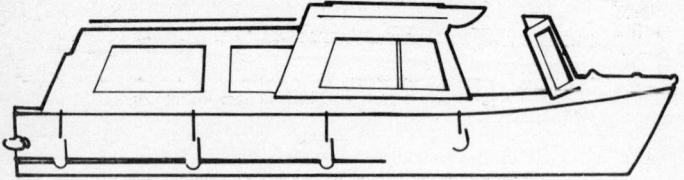

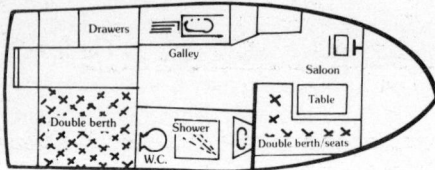

cabin right aft is roomier — it even has a double bunk — but
getting dressed in it means taking turns with your partner.
There are always the convertible settees in the saloon if you
get fed up.

It is just as well you took the hire company's advice and
brought less luggage than you normally take on holiday,
including the uncrushable kind of clothes. Stowage space can
be tight. What you took for a pair of wardrobes proves to be
the tiny loo and cramped shower.

A dreary picture? Not really. One of the wonders of any
small hire craft is how it seems to get bigger inside once you
adjust to its different style and learn how to concentrate your
movements and needs. For most it takes just a day or two. By
the end of your cruise you will start to wonder why you really
need all that space back home.

The picture I've presented, however, is of one of the
smaller, more traditionally-designed boats. There are a host
of other, roomier types including the modern, 'squarer' craft
with more elbow and headroom. Nautical purists may scoff at
what look like elongated houseboats but their raised cabins
running almost the whole length of the hull with broad
windows providing fine views are certainly more spacious and
easier to move around in. Their long, flat-topped deckheads
also give you much more sunbathing space. Paradoxically,
another kind of craft now commonly revived that also gives
much more space both inside and out is the oldest form of
canal boat — the 'narrow boat'. These re-creations of the
horse-drawn barges have comfortable accommodation and
long, raised cabins for easy movement. They may not look as

Narrow Boat. Sleeps 6–8. Good for families.

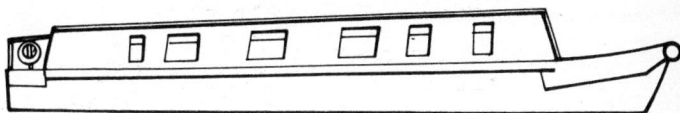

Length 52ft.; beam 6ft. 10ins; headroom 6ft. 2ins.

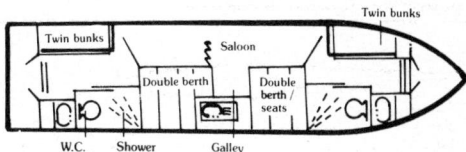

Twin bunks   Twin bunks   Saloon   Double berth   Double berth / seats

W.C.   Shower   Galley

stylish as many of the cruisers for hire but they certainly emphasise the water gypsy effect.

A distinct plus for both these 'squarer' types is that they have larger galleys and boast a full-size cooker, roomy sink, food storage and very adequate fridge as well as sufficient preparation space. There are other kinds of craft that also offer such advantages but not all are as well equipped and it is important when choosing a hire boat to pay close attention to the descriptions given in the brochures. A layout of each craft is nearly always provided and it is fairly simple to work out the size of the galley. Pay particular attention to the location of the galley in relation to the saloon, sleeping cabins, loo, etc. Some boats have the galley squeezed into more inconvenient positions, sometimes down a short flight of steps that make carrying food a bit tricky.

It's difficult to avoid cooking smells in any boat but plenty of ventilation, facilitated by galleys with big windows that open, is important. A number of cruisers have the galley right inside the main cabin, which is convenient for serving up meals but may be hot and smelly for the diners. Also remember that most saloons serve as sleeping areas (using convertible benches) so allow time for smells to clear before turning in for the night. Wherever the galley is situated I recommend ones that are not made difficult for the cook by other crew members constantly squeezing past.

Variations in space are the main differences in most galleys. Most have similar fittings although cookers and fridges can vary in size. Cookers may have two, three or even four rings plus grill and reasonable-size oven. They are run off gas (the Calor Gas kind) and I should underline here that great care is taken by the hire firms to ensure their safety. Most people will have read of alarming tragedies resulting from faulty fittings in boats that have led to a gas build-up of explosive proportions. But these are very rare and British boat companies have an excellent reputation for safety. But take great care yourself.

You will also find the galley well stocked with all the pots, pans and incidental equipment you will need for your holiday (big casserole dishes and steamers are not usually supplied). There is, of course, adequate crockery and cutlery. I should also mention that there is running hot as well as cold water in the sink (and in the wash-basins/shower). This might surprise some who think one really has a very basic lifestyle afloat. Equally you will find your craft fully lit by electricity (operated by the engine that drives the boat). There is also a shaver point and just in case you cannot bear to miss your favourite soap opera many hire craft are supplied with a TV (often colour).

All I have described so far is relevant to cruising abroad as much as in Britain, although you will find that the majority of Continental cruising holidays sold in the UK tend to feature fleets of identically-styled boats according to area. To describe each kind, however, would need a guide all to itself. I have also omitted describing the more nautical features as these are much the same in most craft — usually very simple controls for speed, going astern or ahead, steering, etc. Nearly all craft have a wheel for steering with the main exception being narrow boats where a tiller is used. The control position can be right aft, amidships or even in the bows. What type of craft you choose, however, will probably be decided by the number in your party (from two- to 12-berth boats are available) and the size of your pocket.

3
Waterwise Ways

Every year hundreds of people who hardly know their port from their starboard take boats along waterways for the first time and enjoy a safe holiday — so there should be no reason for you to fear doing exactly the same. The craft are designed for simple operation and as the hire firms all state: 'If you can drive a car you can skipper our boats'. Just to make sure they give you a brief run under instruction before you set out on your own as well as providing you with a handy booklet on all you need to know. However, the basic advice given in this chapter is worth studying before your trip.

RULES OF THE ROAD

Just as on highways there is a correct side to stay on, although there can be variations on some waterways because of particular local circumstances. On narrow canals and small rivers your course is dictated for you but it is vital that you strictly observe local procedures on giving way to oncoming craft. On broader waterways you have to navigate according to buoys and marker posts and you will be given illustrated instructions as to their meaning.

SPEED

It is unlikely your craft can go much faster than around seven knots but even this is too great when passing boats moored to banks and jetties or when passing oncoming craft. Two or three knots' speed will prevent making an uncomfortable wash. Slow down, too, when passing birds nesting as your wash could damage eggs or harm fledglings.

MOORING

You will be given a list of recognised berths for the night or
other longer stays but apply plenty of common sense if
choosing a more independent spot. That empty stretch of
canal bank may look innocent enough but are you going to
tie up alongside a moorhen's nest and frighten it from its
chicks? Or will you block the way for other boats? Do not tie
up to handy posts bearing navigation or warning signs and
thus preventing other skippers seeing them (yes, it does
happen). Make sure you secure mooring ropes carefully to
some solid object and with bends that do not slip but avoid
placing lines across towpaths and other rights of way in case
you inconvenience the public.

LOCKS

Nothing worries first-timers more than the prospect of handling the mechanisms for operating lock gates, especially on
many canals where there could be up to a score of them or
more. But you will have received full advice from the hire
firm on how to raise and lower the gates and you will find it is
a simple business. Some need only one person for the proce-
dure but for others having two could be essential. However,
with the camaraderie that exists among cruise boat hirers
there is nearly always another skipper who will help if you do
get confused. If you, as captain, do it yourself make sure
there is someone competent to handle your craft in and out
of the lock and that they or someone else can safely tackle
the mooring ropes. The bigger locks, such as many found on
the Continent, are usually manned by full-time staff. You can,
of course, always go cruising on a lock-free waterway.

SAFETY PRECAUTIONS

Considering how many novices hire boats there are remarkably few accidents but it pays to take certain precautions.
Extra care is needed when decks get slippery from rain or
spray. Never rush around on deck at any time as it is easy to
trip up on ropes and fixtures. Be careful when stepping
aboard or ashore since boats can suddenly rise and fall or
move sideways without warning. Always choose moorings
where you can keep your craft close alongside. Do not allow
young children to go helter-skelter around the boat or lean
over the side (actually this is just as dangerous when moored
since the boat could suddenly bang against a jetty and crush

limbs). I have rarely heard of youngsters getting into much trouble and I find they make very good crew. But think carefully about taking aged and infirm parents. Getting them on and off boats can pose problems.

CLOTHING

Casual wear, needless to say, is appropriate — and the kind that can be crammed in grips and tight stowage spaces without ironing. Most boats only have a small hanging cupboard with enough room for the odd dress and pair of slacks. Include a warm woollie or two as even in warmer Continental lands it can sometimes get quite chilly on the water at night. Outerwear is important. An anorak, preferably the more waterproof kind, is essential. Steering the boat in an open cockpit or tying up in the rain could soak you and you may have to walk some distance for the groceries when it is wet. For the same reason a pair of wellies is useful but for normal footwear on board, non-slip shoes are vital (no high heels, please). Allow for the fact that there is no washing machine in the craft, although you may well moor in a town with a launderette. Those handy tubes of washing liquid sold for camping are useful if you fancy washing clothes in the sink or a bucket. You will certainly need to do this if a baby is part of the complement.

SWIMMING

It is a constant temptation, especially for children, to dive in whatever waterway you are cruising on. However, it isn't always advisable in view of the risks from passing cruisers and many rivers and canals contain thick, entangling weeds. Boats also tend to leak some oil and petrol in the water. Be patient and wait until you find some safe bywater or deep curve in the bank where it is clean and safe. Better still, seek local knowledge of the safest places to swim. If you do take the plunge do so away from wildlife. Except in the few, rare instances where cruising takes you into the sea or really deep water it is not essential that anyone aboard should be able to swim but it is often recommended by hire firms that half those on board should be capable of doing so.

FISHING

A light line and tackle is always a useful extra and if you do not have any the boat company often hires them out. Fish, however, tend to keep away from busy waterways and it is better to explore a little further afield for good waters. Make sure you get a fishing licence where necessary and do not trespass on private reaches.

PETS

Most boat hire firms allow pets aboard their craft (the conventional kind, at least), although taking a Great Dane or other large animal would present obvious problems. Only you can tell if your Fido would have the sense not to jump overboard. Generally, most dogs do take to boating. There are several cautions to observe such as keeping dogs from barking and annoying other boat users at night and preventing them from chasing farm animals or wildlife. Stop them from diving in fast-flowing waters and make sure you exercise them ashore once a day. I have known owners take cats (even pet mice) but felines do have a habit of wandering long distances in the country. Quarantine regulations forbid bringing animals back into the UK without them going into quarantine for six months.

EXCURSIONS

Most hirers find it a refreshing change to take a day or few hours off to tour the countryside or visit places of interest. It pays to plan your boat trip over a route that carries you close to centres that hold special interest for you and your family or friends. Most hire companies provide a list of interesting places to visit such as historic buildings, theme parks and sports centres. If they are too far for walking consider hiring bicycles — something several boat operators can provide (bikes can be stowed on deck).

ENTERTAINMENT

You'll be surprised just how interested you remain in simply watching the passing scene when cruising but it is vital for rainy days to have something to occupy you (and particularly children) if encased in the small saloon. Books, cards and fold-away games are standard choices and if these pall most craft have TV and/or radio. Also take some favourite sports equipment (tennis rackets?) or just a ball for kicking around if you feel in need of exercise.

YOUR CAR

Most boat hirers travel by car to the cruising base even when it is on the Continent (the holiday operator will include ferry arrangements) as this is more practical for carrying the extra gear you often need. Vehicles can be parked without charge at the bases. When boats are left at a different place to the starting point, your car can often be delivered to it by the hire firm for a reasonable extra charge.

HEALTH

On nearly all waterways you are never that far from a doctor or chemist but getting to them could prove very inconvenient if your boat is not moored close to some town. Take some basic medications like pain-killers, dyspepsia tablets, antiseptic ointments and insect bite sprays. Some craft carry first-aid boxes, but not all, and if you have something similar at home or normally carry one in your car then take that. Sooner or later you or the children will get bumps and scratches in the alien surroundings of a boat. I doubt, however, if you need take seasick pills. If cruising abroad you may feel it wiser to take special medicines prescribed by a doctor rather than chance ones obtained locally. In hot climates carry sunburn lotions and remedies for stomach upsets.

INSURANCE

Virtually all holiday boat companies offer travel insurance that also includes cancellation cover. Most will provide car breakdown and recovery insurance; if not, the motoring organisations offer this type of cover. In Britain the need for extensive cover for doctors and hospitalisation is less necessary than it may be for cruising in some foreign lands. However, there is a Ministry of Health leaflet available which tells you where there are reciprocal national health facilities on the Continent and the procedures necessary. A number of UK private insurance firms offer very comprehensive cover for travel abroad. You may feel it wise to buy fuller cover for the boat itself since the hire firms usually only provide third party insurance. They also insist on you making a damage or accident deposit, which they draw on if you do run into trouble. This may, however, not be sufficient to cover a really bad problem.

EXTRA INFORMATION

If you need to learn more about waterways in Britain and
holiday operators on them the following are useful sources:
British Waterways Board, Melbury House, Melbury Terrace,
London NW16JX (tel: 01262 6711); Inland Waterways
Association, 114 Regents Park Rd, London NW1 8UQ (tel:
01586 2556); and Inland Waterways Protection Society Ltd,
69 Ivy Rd, Macclesfield, Cheshire SK11 8QM (tel: 0625
23595). National tourist offices for the various countries
(addresses are given in the sections devoted to each area) are
also good sources.

4

Waterways Catering

Many people setting out on their first inland cruise looking for new holiday horizons all too often take a foreshortened view where catering on boats is concerned. It will be a picnic alright, they tell themselves — one long picnic from start to end with snacks and cold meals the whole time. But the reality proves different.

In the first place who wants a week, let alone a fortnight, of fish fingers, hamburgers, bacon and eggs and packet soups? Secondly, you will find the crew working up really healthy appetites with boat handling to carry out in all that fresh air. And the alternative of eating ashore isn't always convenient when you are tied up for the night on some lonely reach.

What will encourage the cook to try preparing something more substantial is that in many modern cruisers the stove is often as good as the one in his or her own kitchen at home. They are equipped with three, if not four, rings, a handy-sized oven plus a grill. There is no reason at all why you cannot turn out the chops and two or three vegetables, roast chicken or a joint of beef, even if it has to come without the Yorkshire Pud.

Extra ingenuity and imagination may be called for where there is a shortage of space for storing the range of food-stuffs you are normally used to having and the recipes given are intended to help achieve menu variety. When cruising abroad you may also have to use items of a more alien cuisine. Again some foreign recipes are included in the appropriate area sections.

A certain lack of space for preparing complex dishes may be an inhibition but who wants to slave over a hot cooker on holiday all that much anyway? If you take note of the following basic rules and tips you should succeed without much difficulty.

ON-BOARD TIPS

Choose dishes that do not need very much cooking time. Not only do you want to avoid sacrificing your valuable leisure but it is important you prevent saloons that tend to get warm anyway from becoming overheated. An exception may be an occasional roast on a low-medium heat that can be left to itself most of the time.

Select foodstuffs that do not have too pungent a cooking smell. It can cling to every corner of a small boat. This means most kinds of fish are excluded as are curries and other spicy items.

Make more use of foil-wrapping when cooking, especially on smaller stoves. It is one way of handling more than one item per utensil (putting vegetables into plastic bags for boiling is another) and using aluminium foil as underlay on grills and in the oven can save on cleaning. A lot of foil-wrapped food can be prepared on the grill.

When buying fresh foods such as meat and any frozen items make sure they will all go into the fridge on board. Not only is space limited, there is usually no freezer compartment — the boat's generator isn't capable of providing enough power. It is important that all fresh foods are well protected as they tend to go off rapidly in the craft's warm interior and waterways always seem to attract plenty of flies.

Leave space in the fridge, too, for salads and salad stuffs. These will form a good part of your meals, especially in countries like France where there is such a good choice of ingredients. To avoid boring repetition you will need to use more imagination and I've included several suggestions for brighter salads among the recipes.

Always have a reasonable choice of tinned goods and preserves that do not need special storing. Not only are they useful when other foods run out (you did choose to go hiking rather than shopping!) but can make tasty main meals from choice, as some of the recipes listed suggest. A can opener is usually provided by the boat company.

Since you always have to buy milk daily (no milkman calling) a tin or jar of the dried kind is a handy standby. And do not forget to have plenty of cooking oil as many of the simpler dishes suited to boat catering are cooked in it.

WHAT FOOD TO TAKE WITH YOU

Although most hire firms will accept grocery orders in advance so that you have some essentials waiting aboard to cover needs for the first day or two (most cruises start over weekends), you may well prefer to take some items with you from home. As the majority of hirers travel to their craft by car there is usually space for a box of foodstuffs.

The advantages of pre-buying are that you can choose just the brands and sizes you prefer — important if cruising abroad where the goods are unfamiliar — plus you can take a number of items not included in the advance shopping list you are sent. But do not overdo the amount as storage space aboard is limited.

Most of the groceries will have to be tinned, preserved or otherwise suitable for carrying a good distance in a car boot. You can include vacuum-packed foods such as bacon and sausages, although the importation of such items may be prohibited in some countries (check with the hire company or national tourist office).

Suitable goods include: tinned meats, fish, soups, pastas, baked beans and other vegetables; instant and packaged items such as soups, dessert mixes, sauces, gravy granules, potatoes, dried vegetables and spaghetti. Also useful are tinned fruit, biscuits, crispbread, cereals, coffee, tea, marmalade, jams, salad cream and bottled sauces. Vegetarians and health food consumers can also include a good range of soya-based products. Sugar- or salt-free foodstuffs not always easily available abroad can also be added if required. It is worth emphasising that anyone needing special dietary food for medical reasons should either take such items with them when cruising abroad or try to ascertain through the hire firm or tourist office if they are available (and their foreign names) in the particular country.

If you are flying or going by some other means of transport then the quantity of food you can take will be very restricted but I certainly suggest when going overseas you try and squeeze in your favourite marmalade, coffee and tea. A familiar start to the day more quickly helps you adjust to foreign surroundings and food later on.

EQUIPMENT TO TAKE

All craft are equipped with crockery, cutlery, glasses and kitchen utensils needed for the number of persons aboard. Yet there are some useful, extra items worth taking if space is available in your vehicle. These include:

Picnic basket fitted with crockery and cutlery.

Plastic containers for keeping food fresher, including bottles for soft drinks and milk.

Aluminium foil for wrapping food both for picnics and for cooking aboard.

Insulated ice boxes. The chemical packs that accompany these need to be frozen and most shop owners with a deep freeze will co-operate in doing this.

Two vacuum flasks for keeping drinks both cool and warm.

Cooking equipment. Some keen cruiser fans I know like to take some handy extra items along — such as those easily adjustable steamers that fit into any size pan. They help you cook more than one vegetable or other foodstuff at a time on small stoves. Your galley may not have a decent size casserole dish and these can prove very useful. A hand whisk (the boat's electricity cannot cope with the electric kind) is another useful item not always found aboard.

Baby gear. Not every boat company can provide the special chairs or other equipment that babes in arms need. There may also be nowhere suitable for fixing a harness. It is best if you check with the hirer as to what can be provided or what is most suitable for you to bring. Take baby's feeding mug and an unbreakable plastic bowl or two. Don't forget the baby food.

One obvious item that should be taken but is often forgotten is a good, strong carrier bag with easy-grip handles for bringing the shopping back to the craft. There may often be a long walk and plastic bags are not the best thing to use. A rucksack is a good substitute.

SHOPPING ON HOLIDAY

Although most waterways run through towns or large villages where you can easily shop you are limited by the small amount you can safely keep on board. Fresh items may necessitate you shopping every one or two days. Planning main dishes several days ahead helps concentrate the mind on essentials. Also remember the items you will need for canal or riverside bank picnics.

Meats: Smaller, easily cooked kinds are best, including chicken portions, chops and steaks. Minced meat is also useful for simple dishes like spaghetti bolognese. Meat pies are alright if eaten at once and if storage is difficult some tinned pies and other meats can be attractively served up. Buy cooked meats for snacks and picnics.

Vegetables: With the exception of root crops such as potatoes and carrots most vegetables will have to be bought daily or thereabouts. Avoid cabbage for boiling, though, as this will really smell you out on deck. Buy plenty of salad stuff. When cruising in warmer countries you must include items such as aubergines and artichokes that are cheap compared with the price in Britain and add considerably to the variety of meals afloat. Olives and some tasty (but not too smelly) foreign kinds of onions are also musts.

Fruit/Cheese: Leave plenty of space in your bag for fruit. In my experience a hungry crew can eat every apple, orange and pear in sight. Fruit is also useful in varying salads. On many waterways you may find yourself cruising right through orchards, strawberry and raspberry fields where the fruit is much cheaper than in the shops. On the Continent you may tie up alongside a vineyard for fresh grapes. Tinned fruit, however, is an essential standby at non-fruiting seasons. Cheese is one of the more useful snack items but the hard kind is better because cheese sweats easily aboard a boat. Softer French cheeses need to go in the fridge, even if this upsets the purists.

Drinks: Canned beers will store best and are handiest for drinking while underway. Ensure plenty of soft drinks for the children who are always demanding them. Carry a bottle or two of wine (the fridge may only take one or two for chilling); take spirits, too, but you'll find yourself passing enough pubs, bars or *estaminets* to satisfy every kind of thirst.

PART II

INLAND
WATERWAYS:

CRUISING REGIONS

5
British Isles

ENGLAND AND WALES

Believe it or not but there are over 2,000 miles (3,200 km) of cruising waterways in England and Wales. With a remarkable variety, they range from busier waters like the Thames to wild, marshy area such as the Lincolnshire Fens; from hidden canals on Welsh mountainsides to canals passing through big industrial cities. They stretch from as far south as Kent and Somerset to North Yorkshire; from the North Sea to the Irish Sea and the Bristol Channel; through the rugged Pennines or like a spider's web across the flat Norfolk Broads.

It would be possible, given time, to make a round voyage of much of the two countries using the interlocking system of rivers and canals but for just a week or a fortnight one must choose a particular area, and since your craft moves slowly and temptations to stop are great, your choice needs to be fairly concentrated. Scenery is a useful yardstick in making a decision. Lovers of truly rural surroundings can choose the plentiful waterways of Shropshire, Worcestershire and Staffordshire, the Severn Valley or the Thames along its upper reaches. Flat earthers have a rich choice in East Anglia while those wanting more rugged scenery can find it in Lancashire and Yorkshire on the Leeds-Liverpool Canal. The Midlands should satisfy industrial heritage enthusiasts.

Hire craft bases are well sprinkled around the countryside, offering routes both long and short. Shorter waterways may well suit first-timers seeking a trial holiday, especially several detached ones like the Lancaster, River Medway and Brecon and Abergavenny Canal. The Norfolk and Suffolk Broads are also good areas for sampling inland cruising. The bolder traveller can combine two or more systems, for example linking the Grand Union artery with some of the connecting veins or crossing from the Midlands right into North Wales

England's Holiday Waterways

LAKE WINDERMERE
Tewitfield
Lancaster
LANCASTER CANAL
LIVERPOOL LEEDS & CANAL
RIVER URE
RIVER FOSS
RIVER DERWENT
RIVER OUSE
RIVER HULL
SELBY CANAL
AIRE AND CALDER CANAL
Burnley
Leeds
Liverpool
BRIDGWATER CANAL
SHEFFIELD & S. YORKS. CANAL
RIVER ANCHOLME
MACCLESFIELD CANAL
CHESTERFIELD CANAL
FOSSDYKE CANAL
CROMFORD CANAL
LLANGOLLEN CANAL
TRENT & MERSEY CANAL
RIVER TRENT
Nottingham
NORFOLK & SUFFOLK BROADS
King's Lynn
SHROPSHIRE UNION CANAL
ASHBY CANAL
GRAND UNION CANAL
RIVER NENE
Peterborough
RIVER WISSEY
BIRMINGHAM CANAL NAVIGATIONS
Birmingham
RIVER LITTLE OUSE
STAFFORDSHIRE WORCESTER & BIRMINGHAM CANAL
Coventry
Northampton
Cambridge
Bedford
RIVER LARK
RIVER CAM
STRATFORD-ON-AVON CANAL
RIVER SEVERN
Gloucester
RIVER AVON
OXFORD CANAL
GRAND UNION CANAL
Bishop's Stortford
CHELMER & BLACKWATER CANAL
GLOUCHESTER & SHARPNESS CANAL
RIVER THAMES
Oxford
RIVER LEE
London
RIVER ROACH
Bath
RIVER AVON
RIVER KENNET
RIVER THAMES
RIVER MEDWAY
Maidstone
Bridgwater
RIVER PARRET
KENNET & AVON CANAL
RIVER WEY
Guildford
Tonbridge
WEY & ARUN CANAL
RIVER ARUN
BRIDGWATER & TAUNTON CANAL

along the fascinating Llangollen Canal. The latter, although fairly short, emphasises the remarkable variety to be found, even on just one waterway. After crossing the Cheshire Plains you ascend by means of several lift bridges until you are clinging to the contours high above the River Dee. In the process you cross impressive aqueducts such as Telford's masterpiece, the breathtaking Pontcysyllte, 1,000 feet long and 120 feet high (300 × 36 m). On many canals you pass through mountainside tunnels while others lie almost hidden between fields, orchards and woods. There is no better way of seeing England and Wales at their most beautiful or most historic — many of our finest cathedrals, stately homes and oldest industrial sites stand on canal or river banks or close by.

The comparative narrowness of waterways in England and Wales means your speed rarely exceeds more than six or seven knots and the average daily distance covered is usually 20 miles. Another limitation is that on many routes you have to return the way you came. But there are several hire companies that allow boats to be left at a destination terminus and there are some more closely interknit networks, such as the Broads and Midlands canals and rivers, where a circular cruise is possible.

Cruise companies

There are numerous hire companies, from major tour operators with very big fleets who market their countrywide holidays extensively to those with a small number of craft based at just one centre for local use. A full list of operators would be far too great to include here and you can find this in the very useful *Inland Waterways Guide* published annually by the Inland Waterways Association in conjunction with Brittain Publications (£1.95). Write to the Association at 114 Regent's Park Rd, London NW1 8UQ (tel: 01 586 2510). The following are three of the larger firms offering hire over a wide area.

Blakes, Wroxham, Norwich NR12 8DH (tel: 0533 701701)

Hoseasons Holidays, Sunway House, Lowestoft, Suffolk NR32 3LT (tel: 0502 87373)

Boat Enquiries Ltd, 43 Botley Rd, Oxford OX2 0PT (tel: 0865 727288)

Sources of useful information

British Waterways Board, Melbury House, Melbury Terrace, London NW1 6JX (tel: 01 262 6711)

Inland Waterways Protection Society, 69 Ivy Rd, Macclesfield, Cheshire SK11 8QM (tel: 0625 23595)

Inland Waterways Association (address above)

English Tourist Board, Thames Tower, Black's Rd, Hammersmith, London W6 9EL (tel: 01 846 9000)

Any of the many regional tourist information offices throughout the country will supply information.

SCOTLAND

The rest of Great Britain may have plenty of man-made waterways but nowhere is there so much natural cruising opportunity as in Scotland. Its hundreds of miles of both inland and sheltered sea lochs provide unrivalled routes for an uncrowded holiday afloat with easy navigation — and all in beautiful scenery. Pretty well all the hire craft waters lie in the Highlands or close by, belying their name but gaining from their magnificent scenery.

Inland you can cruise historic Loch Lomond or you can

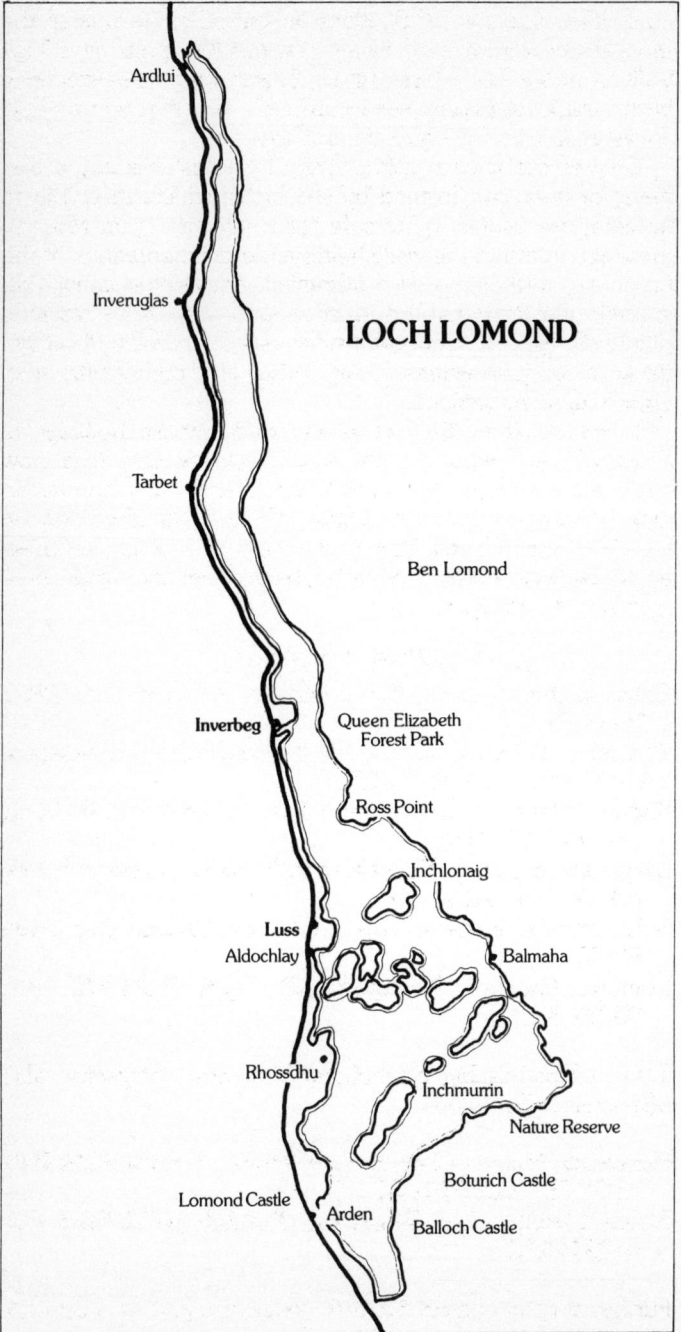

LOCH LOMOND

Ardlui

Inveruglas

Tarbet

Ben Lomond

Inverbeg

Queen Elizabeth
Forest Park

Ross Point

Inchlonaig

Luss
Aldochlay

Balmaha

Rhossdhu

Inchmurrin

Nature Reserve

Boturich Castle

Lomond Castle

Arden

Balloch Castle

cross from one side of Scotland to the other on one of the most popular routes of all — between Inverness and Fort William along Loch Ness (the monster hasn't attacked any boats yet), over other less-famous lochs and through the few 'locks' that form the Caledonian Canal.

One of the special attractions of Scottish waters is that many of them are formed by sea lochs, which, in spring to autumn, are usually quite safe for small hire craft. Most of these are found in the well sheltered deep indentations of the Clyde or further up the adjoining Argyllshire coast. No special qualifications are needed and hire firms provide plenty of easily understood instructions for handling boats in these more open waters. Your cruiser also comes with adequate safety equipment.

In recent times the organising of waterway holidays in Scotland has become much more efficient and it is now much easier to book your craft there. A special organisation called Scottish Holidays Afloat, Marine Parade, Dundee DD1 3JD (tel: 0382 21555), has been set up to centralise bookings. It also distributes full details of member firms, their craft and the charges.

Cruise companies

Caley Cruisers, Canal Rd, Inverness IV3 6NF (tel: 0463 236328)

Cameron Cruisers, Onich, Fort William, Inverness-shire PH33 6RY (tel: 085 53 224)

Highland Holiday Boats, Dochgarroch, Inverness IV3 6JX (tel: 0463 86 265)

Largs Cruisers, Largs Yacht Haven, Irvine Rd, Largs, Ayrshire (tel: 0475 675625)

Solas Marine, Banavie Top Lock, Fort William (tel: 0396 5305)

Lomond Charters, Lochgoilhead, Argyll PA24 8AE (tel: 03013 382)

Two of Britain's biggest holiday boat hire companies also offer craft in Scotland.

Hoseasons Holidays Ltd, Sunway House, Lowestoft, Suffolk NR32 3LT (tel: 0502 87373)

Blakes Holidays Ltd, Wroxham, Norwich NR12 8DH (tel: 06053 3223)

Further information on Scottish waterways and the country's tourist attractions can be obtained from:

Scottish Tourist Board, 23 Ravelston Terrace, Edinburgh
  EH4 3EU (tel: 031-225 2424). The London office is at 5
  Pall Mall East, London SW1Y 5BA (tel: 01 980 8661)
Highlands and Islands Development Board, 27 Bank St,
  Inverness IV1 1QR (tel: 0463 34171)

IRELAND

Lakes and rivers ignore man-made boundaries and where
cruising on them in Ireland is concerned it is better to ignore
the political division between Ulster and the Republic. One of
the leading waterways, the Erne, although mainly in the
North, has joining points both sides of the border. If nature
goes its own way there you can follow suit and do not get put
off by the alarming events of so many years past: many
hundreds from the British mainland and abroad go cruising
on the Erne without trouble. Its peaceful tranquillity is, in fact,
one of its greatest attractions.

The other of the two major inland boating waters in
Ireland is that mighty stretch known as the Shannon, which is
navigable for 140 miles (225 km with only six locks) running
south from close to the Ulster border along the Republic's
western side. There is a third route, the Grand Canal, lying
east-west from close to Dublin with a connecting arm down
the Barrow River.

The Erne

This 50 mile-long (80 km) waterway actually covers 300
square miles (480 sq km) of water being formed mainly by
two large lakes, Lower and Upper Erne. They offer two
distinct faces — the former being broader while the latter is a
maze of channels and islands (an easily followed marker
system makes navigation simple). They are joined by the
River Erne at the midway point where the pleasant town of
Fermanagh stands. Elsewhere, wildlife, especially birds, is
abundant and there are several interesting small harbours. A
big attraction, particularly for anyone wanting to play Swiss
Family Robinson, are the many small islands. On some you
can picnic, but watch out for the goats that have gone wild
on a few of these thickly green atolls. There should be little
problem catching your supper as fish, including some big
specimens, abound.

You can join your hire craft at several handy points — at
either end or mid-way along the system. Leading hire firms
are:

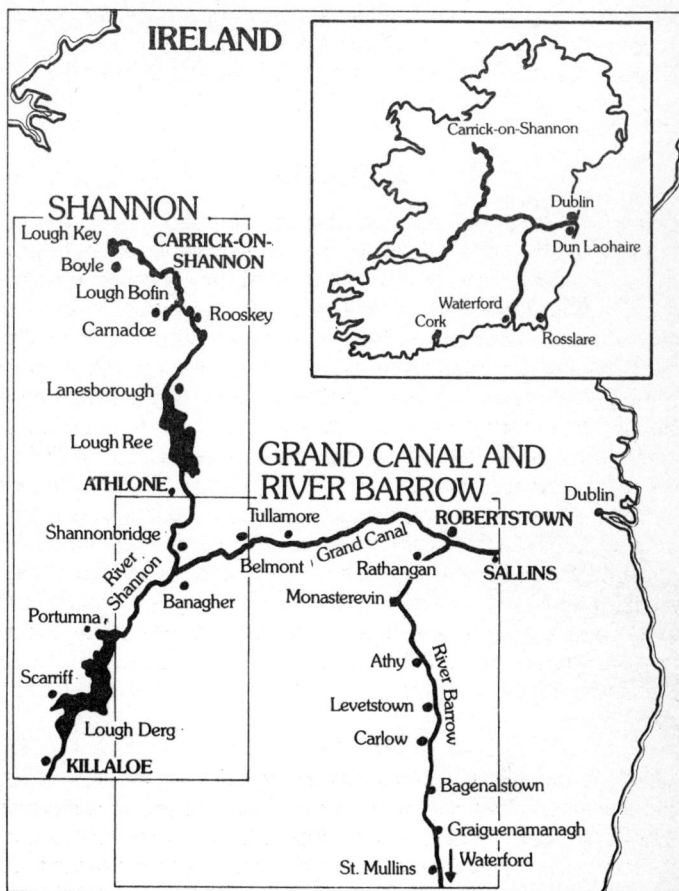

Erne Marine, Bellanaleck, Enniskillen (tel: 036582 267)

Lakeland Marina, Muckross, Kesh, Co. Fermanagh (tel: 036 56 31414)

Manor House Marine, Killadeas, Co. Fermanagh (tel: 036 56 21561)

Aghinver Boat Co, Lisnarick, Co. Fermanagh (tel: 036 56 31400)

Crannog Cruising, Bellanaleck, Enniskillen (tel: 036582 349)

Carrybridge Boat Co, Lesbellaw, Co. Fermanagh (tel: 0365 87651)

Lochside Cruisers, Tempo Rd, Enniskillen (tel: 0365 24368)

Book-a-Boat Ltd, Belturbet, Co. Cavan, Eire (tel: 049 22147)

All the above companies are members of the Erne Charter Boat Association. Its brochure, containing all necessary information, including types of craft and charges, can be obtained from the Northern Ireland Tourist Board, 48 High St, Belfast BT1 2DS (tel: 0232 231221), which will also provide much other useful data about the country.

Shannon

This river-lake chain running through two-thirds of western Eire contains the largest area of inland water in the British Isles. Its popularity can be judged from the fact that around 475 hire boats are operated along it by nine companies. Because of the great area, however, there are no crowded sections. Nor are there any big, busy centres — mostly small villages and towns. You certainly get close to nature but you can get some way from land crossing the two big lakes, Lough Derg and Lough Ree. These are large enough for warnings to be made about risking choppy waters in strong winds.

It can take about a fortnight to make a round trip, keeping to a suitably slow Irish speed and much of the fun consists of idling the time away in the many local bars and joining in their organised sing-songs. Good angling can also slow you down. Many hirers prefer to explore just one section at a time and you can join boats at bases the whole length of the waterway. Carrick-on-Shannon at the northern end, Athlone in the centre, and Killaloe at the southern extremity are popular joining points but the remainder can be equally handy. Some companies permit craft to be left at points different from the starting one. The nine hire companies are:

Emerald Star Line, 37 Dawson St, Dublin 2 (tel: 01 718870)
Flagline (1972) Ltd, Shancurragh, Athlone, Co. Westmeath (tel: 0902 72892)
SGS (Marine) Ltd, Ballykeeran, Athlone, Co. Westmeath (tel: 0902 85163)
Carrick Craft, PO Box 14, Reading RG3 6TA (tel: 0734 22975)
Athlone Cruisers Ltd, Shancurragh, Athlone, Co. Westmeath (tel: 0902 72892)
Silverline Cruisers Ltd, Banagher, Co. Offaly (tel: 0902 51112)
Shannon Castle Line, Dolphin Works, Ringsend, Dublin 4 (tel: 01 600964)
Atlantis Marine Ltd, Parks Marine Centre, Killaloe, Co. Clare (tel: 061 76281)
Derg Line Cruisers, Killaloe, Co. Clare (tel: 061 76364)

Note: Phone calls to the Irish Republic must be prefixed as follows: 0001 for Dublin; 010 353 (you omit the 0 preceding the local number) for other parts of the country. Some Irish exchanges are not automatic exchanges so you will have to dial the operator (100).

Full details of hiring can be obtained by applying to the Irish Tourist Board for its special fact sheet: 150 New Bond St, London W1Y 0AQ (tel: 01 493 3201). It also has offices in Birmingham (6 Temple Row, B2 5HG, tel: 021 236 9724); Manchester (28 Cross St, M2 3NH, tel: 061 832 5981); and Glasgow (19 Dixon St, G1 4AJ, tel: 041 221 2311).

Grand Canal/River Barrow

Although it is one of the oldest canals in the British Isles — built in the eighteenth century between Dublin and the Shannon, connecting part way with the Barrow leading to the port of Waterford — it is little known in the UK. Yet it has great charm and scenic interest, passing through some lovely Midland countryside. You join your craft, which are tourist versions of the old narrow boats, at Lucan, just west of the capital and travel 80 miles (128 km) through 24 locks to the Shannon. Near the midway mark, at Robertstown, you can divert down the Barrow, one of Ireland's prettiest rivers.

One hire firm, Celtic Canal Cruisers, Tullamore, Co. Offaly (tel: 0506 21861), provides boats for two to seven persons. See details under Shannon for further information from the tourist board.

Shopping

Don't be put off if you cannot always find what looks like a grocery shop. Quite often you can buy a whole range of basic items in bars, sweetshops and even ironmongers. Those small village shops often stay open all hours. Equally they may be easygoing about when they open. Stocking up well before beginning the cruise (hire firms will place groceries aboard) is advisable.

The types and brands of foodstuffs in the Republic closely follow the British pattern although sausages can be spicier and bacon smokier. Fresh fish is not all that common in the south. Do try some of the special Irish breads, particularly in the north. Most Ulster towns have their own bakery and a speciality are 'farls' that usually come in triangular shapes, are baked on a griddle and are made with soda, butter and milk but not yeast. You can get treacle, soda, potato and even heather farls. Soda bread is also common in the Republic as are 'bracks', a type of fruit loaf.

Eating Out

Many pubs in Ulster and a growing number in the south serve tasty lunches and snacks. Seafood, including local oysters and eels, is a particularly popular item in the north; also try the Guinness and oyster soup served up there. Before eating out on your Erne cruise get the *Let's Eat Out In Northern Ireland* booklet listing over 1,000 eating spots (available from newsagents and tourist information centres). The Irish Tourist Board also publishes a useful fact sheet.

If there is a marked difference between holidaying in the Republic and in Ulster it is cost. While most things in Northern Ireland are similar in price to the mainland (even cheaper), those in Eire are often noticeably more expensive, even allowing for a slightly better pound sterling to 'Punt' rate. If you are going over by car it pays to take some provisions with you.

RECIPES

The following are a few of the simple but tasty, satisfying dishes that can be prepared in a small galley wherever you go cruising. These particularly apply on the inland waters of the British Isles. There is a special section of foreign recipes you may wish to try out on the spot at the end of each country's description. In general, recipes here are for 3-4 people.

Eggs Supreme

1 packet quick-cook rice   *1 medium-size tin of cream*
1 hard boiled egg per person   *of mushroom soup*
Shrimps or tinned fish   *paprika*

Place boiled rice on serving dish with eggs halved in centre. Pour heated soup into which fish and shrimps have been added over rice and eggs. Sprinkle paprika on top.

Pan Haggerty

1 lb (500g) potatoes   *Salt and pepper*
½lb (250g) onions
¼lb (120g) cheese (cheddar
  or similar)

Slice potatoes, onions and cheese thinly and place in alternate layers in a well-oiled frying pan seasoning each layer with salt and pepper. Cover with lid and cook gently for around half an hour until tender. You can also add bacon, sausages, ham and other cooked meats.

Beef Rice Spanish Style

¼lb (120g) long grain rice	level teaspoon salt
1oz (30g) butter or	1 green pepper
margarine	1 rounded teaspoon castor
1 medium size onion	sugar
½lb (250g) minced beef	Parmesan cheese
1 large tin tomatoes	

Sprinkle rice in pan of boiling water and cook quickly for 8-10 minutes before draining. Melt butter or margarine in saucepan and add sliced onion. Fry over moderate heat until golden brown. Add beef and brown. Stir in tomatoes, salt, sliced green pepper and sugar and then add cooked rice. Cover with lid and simmer for 30 minutes stirring occasionally. Grate cheese on top.

Chicken or Turkey Breast Continental

Brush individual breasts with oil or melted butter or margarine. Season with salt and pepper and sprinkle with parsley or tarragon. Seal well in tin foil and cook for 20 minutes. Serve with rice, vegetables or salad.

Fruit Fritters

Make a batter from two-thirds of a cup of milk or water to a cup of plain flour. Add 2 tablespoons of oil and 2 eggs, pinch of salt (and sugar if desired). Beat vigorously until smooth. Leave for half an hour.

Fruit can be cored apples sliced in rings, pineapple slices, sliced bananas or oranges, apricot halves or even berries. Marinate them in wine or sweet liquor for 1 hour. Drain well before dipping in batter evenly. Fry until browned.

Banana Fool

2 bananas	2 level tablespoons
lemon juice	custard powder
½ pint (¼l) milk	1oz (30g) castor sugar

Mash bananas in basin with squeeze of lemon juice. Make

thin paste from custard powder with a little milk added. Bring rest of milk to boil in separate pan and stir it into custard paste. Pour it all back into milk pan and bring to boil stirring all the time. Add sugar and cook for 1 minute. Take pan off heat and stir in banana mash. Serve with cream. Other soft fruits make good fools.

6

France

For a country offering so much good wine it is surprising how many holidaymakers take to 'the water' in this delightful country. France is over-blessed with a great range of fine, broad rivers and canals. The numerous waterways on which hire cruising takes place all pass through lovely scenery and charming, often historic, towns and cities. It is hardly any surprise that of all the European countries where Britons go inland voyaging, this one is the most popular.

Added temptations are that it is within easy ferry reach for the majority who take their car and the really choice range of waterside eating places, plus the succulent variety of fresh produce for catering aboard. As there are also plenty of well-organised, easy-to-buy holiday firm deals featuring French cruising there is really no reason for anyone to hesitate.

The only problem is deciding on which attractive waterway to choose. You find organised cruising in most of the favourite tourist regions from the Atlantic *département* of Brittany to the French Mediterranean coast; from Lorraine-Alsace in the north to Bordeaux in the south-west. Central regions are also well covered. It is best, perhaps, if you decide on some particular attraction of each area as a guide.

One outstanding feature in most of the regions is the local wine or spirit. Do you prefer Burgundy to Bordeaux? Cognac to Calvados? You could also have a sparkling cruise through Champagne country. Varieties of French cuisine offer another alternative — the truffles and *pâté de foie gras* of Perigord to the *bordelaise* sauces of Bordeaux; the *crêpes* of Brittany to the *cassoulet* of the Languedoc. However, wherever you cruise, local wines and dishes are excellent.

The type of countryside is another yardstick. Try the mixture of meadow and moorland in Brittany; the more mountainous, wooded scenery of Lorraine-Alsace; the cozy truly rural scenery of Burgundy; or the sweeping valleys of the Loire. History suggests useful trails to follow, such as the home of future kings of England in Plantagenet Anjou, the old Roman cities of the Languedoc, or the seventeenth- and eighteenth-century *châteaux* country. And what about wildlife as a pointer? Well, you find that everywhere, although it is nowhere more evident than cruising through the Camargue, with its wild horses and flocks of pink flamingos.

Perhaps rather more practical considerations might apply. Most beginners to hire cruising may well prefer the narrower rivers, although most French ones are broader than in the UK. Burgundy and Brittany offer some that are suitable. Some bigger canals and rivers carry heavy commercial traffic that calls for greater concentration on navigation. If you do not feel you can handle too many locks, seek waterways with just a few (most French canals have quite a number although they can be well spread out and, in general, they are supervised by lock-keepers). Check with the hire firm first. A number of the routes allow you to make circular cruises while on others you can only go the one way. Sometimes you have to return over the same course but there are others where you can leave your craft at another base.

Whichever you select, forget that the French waterway systems allow you to go further (and sometimes faster) than in Britain or Ireland. There are far too many seductions *en route*, not least the constant array of tempting inns, eating places and lovely picnic spots. Have you ever tied up to a vineyard as a refuelling stop?

Some prospective boat hirers worry that handling craft in France might be more difficult than their experience in the UK. In fact there is virtually no difference. Controls are similar and just as easy to grasp. Some local 'rules of the road' might be different but they are usually the same as in the UK, following international practice. Boat types are much the same — ranging from the conventional motor cruiser to the modern, more blunt-ended and picture-window-style craft. You will even find some similar to British narrow boats. Equally the interior fittings, including the galley, are virtually the same.

The following concise descriptions of waterways cover those areas where British tour operators and hire companies offer holidays. There are a small number of other waterways where craft are available for independent hire.

BRITTANY

This, the easiest to reach by ferry from Britain, has 400 miles (640km) of rivers and canals just inland from the Atlantic. You can cruise from the coast of southern Brittany north to near St Malo or from some inland base anywhere along a four-legged network of waterways going as far south as the old city of Nantes. Much of the scenery is pasture and moor with ancient Breton 'Stonehenges' like Carnac, but there are valleys and forests. Try the *crêpes*, cider and seafood (oysters and giant prawns are a feature).

BRITTANY

FINISTERRE

This less-known cruise region will suit the escapists. It is also ideal for beginners for there is no commercial traffic along much of the waterway, the River Aulne. But there are 31 unmanned locks. You can travel both ways, east and west, from your inland base and heading west brings you right to the Atlantic with the possibility of cruising the sea estuary.

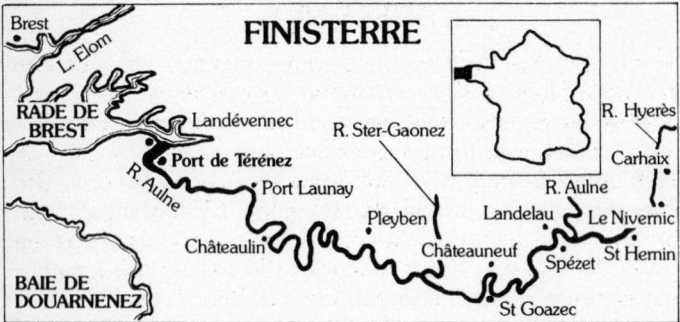

MAINE-ANJOU

British hire firms have only just begun marketing this tucked away region, a little off the main tourist tracks. Again it is an area for leisurely escapists as there is no commercial traffic on the three rivers that form a fairly extensive chain 160 miles (258km) long. Most cruise just sections from the old city of Angers or two other bases. The 25 locks on one river and 20 on another will slow you down a bit. If it's speed you want the 24-hour circuit at Le Mans is at the northern extremity. The Anjou, that genuine rosé wine, is a must and the region's cuisine rates highly.

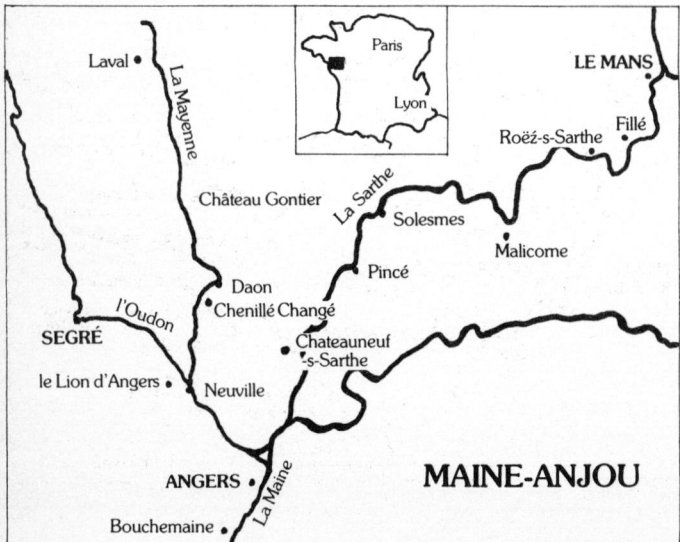

BURGUNDY

No French *département* has a more complex array of hire craft routes than this one. There are several small rivers, parts of those bigger ones the Loire and Rhône, plus six canals. It's best if you choose from four or five separate itineraries — all offer pretty scenery and interesting excursions ashore. The Nivernais Canal route with its 108 miles (174 km) linked with the Loire and taking in lakes and tunnels is popular, as is the Canal de Bourgogne, for along its 150 miles (240 km) lies that centre of *haute cuisine* in France, Dijon. Another route takes in the Yonne and Nivernais rivers from the beautiful town of Auxerre, while a fourth, further east, concentrates on the River Saône but allows several variations on adjoining waterways. Almost anywhere provides several permutations of choice and only time prevents you seeing more than a particular corner. The magnificent choice of wines could dictate your route: Chablis, Chambertin, Beaune, Sancerre, Nuits St George, to mention but a few. It is invidious to mention dishes in this heartland of good food but the *escargots de Bourgogne*, the *charcuterie* and, of course the mustard and Kir from Dijon, should all be tried.

BURGUNDY

LORRAINE-ALSACE

Just why this lovely area with its good waterways should have been left so long before being featured by cruising companies is a mystery except, perhaps, that it lies away from fashionable routes. Yet it is an indication of just how popular French cruising has become that one operator at least now includes it. Its main route is the Canal de la Marne au Rhine with offshoots north and south along two other canals. One can also connect with the Moselle at Nancy. The big attraction lies at the opposite end — the city of Strasbourg with its European parliament. The scenery for much of the way is impressive with thickly wooded slopes, and one can see the former German influence in many of the quaint old towns. Although commercial traffic is carried, the waterway can be more relaxing than many others since the locks are electrically operated. The cuisine is an interesting mix of French and German (try the *choucroute* and fruit tarts) and tasty Alsace wine shares a place with beer.

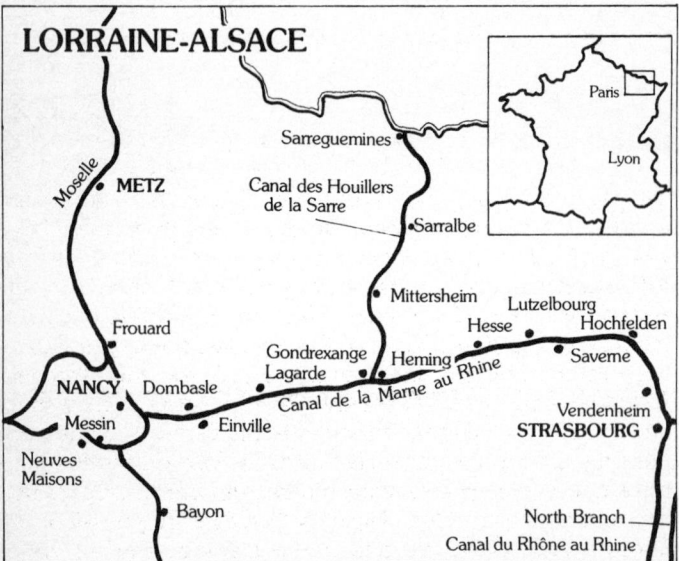

LORRAINE-ALSACE

Paris
Lyon

Moselle
METZ
Sarreguemines
Canal des Houillers
de la Sarre
Sarralbe
Mittersheim
Lutzelbourg
Frouard
Hesse
Hochfelden
Gondrexange
Heming
Saverne
Lagarde
Canal de la Marne au Rhine
NANCY
Dombasle
Vendenheim
Messin
Einville
STRASBOURG
Neuves
Maisons
Bayon
North Branch
Canal du Rhône au Rhine

COGNAC

The name itself should raise your spirits as you cruise from one distillery to another along the 101 miles (162 km) of the River Charente from your inland base to the Atlantic near

Rochefort. It is a very peaceful waterway with no commercial craft — just 21 locks. Very suitable for the really easygoing holidaymaker as the river is slow moving and shallow, and the water is clean enough for swimming. The countryside is charming and little changed for centuries.

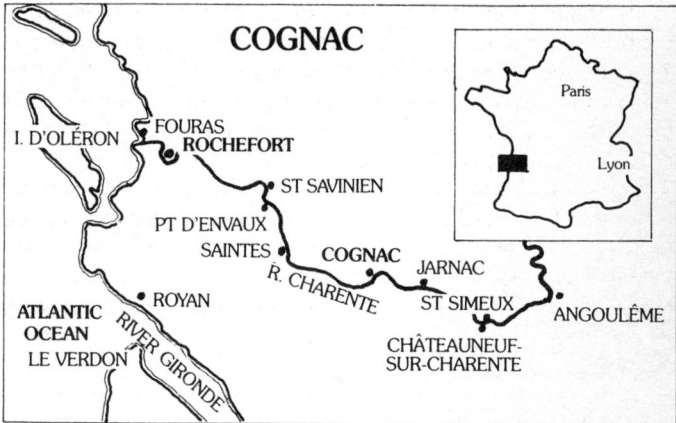

CANAL DU MIDI

This, undoubtedly, is the most impressive of all French cruise waterways, especially when directly linked with the Canal Lateral à la Garonne. Together they form a 350-mile-long (563 km) route right across southern-central France from the Atlantic to the Mediterranean. Not only is it a fine engineering feat, it also offers some of the grandest scenery and loveliest historic towns in the country. Clearly too long to cover its whole length (when combined) in a normal holiday span, cruises on it concentrate on sections. Many take the one from near the city of Toulouse eastwards to Sète on the Mediterranean, a Venice-like seventeenth-century port. *En route* you marvel at such ancient places as Carcassonne, possibly the finest fortified city in Europe, and Agde, the beautiful 'Black Pearl' fishing harbour. Going west along the 'Garonne' you steer through the famous wine country to the city of Bordeaux. Eating out is a special pleasure since there are many canalside restaurants you can try as well as the seafood ones beside the Med.

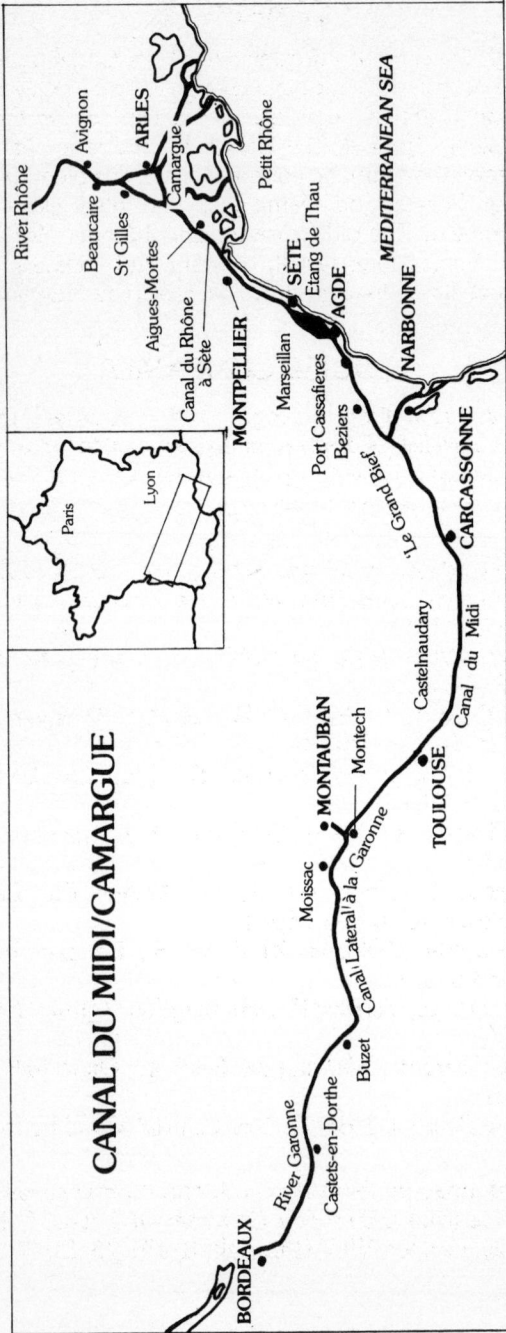

CANAL DU MIDI/CAMARGUE

CAMARGUE

Although the route is an extension of the Canal du Midi it is, because of distance, normally taken separately. One can start from near Agde or begin the cruise right in the Camargue sailing along the lock-free Canal du Rhône à Sète. It runs right beside the dramatic countryside with its plentiful wildlife, including horses and flamingos, and also close by the Mediterranean. The old Crusader city of Aigues Mortes is one landfall. Seafood, especially oysters and mussels, are the local speciality — they go down well with the Muscadet.

CRUISE COMPANIES

Nearly a dozen firms arrange self-drive cruises. These are mainly specialist operators, but include a few conventional tour companies offering a cruise as part of bigger programmes. The list includes:

Blakes Holidays, Wroxham, Norwich (tel: 06053 3224)

Hoseasons Holidays, Sunway House, Lowestoft, Suffolk (tel: 0502 57111)

Blue Line Cruisers, Ferry View Estate, Horning, Norwich (tel: 0692 630128)

French Country Cruises, 10 Barley Mow Passage, London W4 (tel: 01 995 3642)

Slipaway Holidays, 90 Newland Rd, Worthing, Sussex (tel: 0903 213751)

Angel Travel, 47 High St, Tonbridge, Kent (tel: 0732 361115)

Air France Holidays, 69 Boston Manor Rd, Brentford, Middlesex (tel: 01 568 6981)

French Leave Holidays, 21 Fleet St, London EC4 (tel: 01 583 8383)

Golden France, Ferrars Rd, Huntingdon, Cambs (tel: 0480 50017)

Holiday Charente, Wardington, Banbury, Oxon (tel: 029575 8282)

Sunshine Boating, 8 Ber St, Norwich (tel: 0603 630513)

More information about hire craft and on France generally is obtainable from the French Government Tourist Office, 178 Piccadilly, London W1V 0AL (tel: 01 491 7622).

SHOPPING

There are travel buffs who argue that shopping in France these EEC days is not much different from the experience in Britain with many items much the same, including plenty of instant foods that bely the country's *haute cuisine* image. There are also a flourishing number of hypermarkets looking more American than French. Yet there is still a more enticing, sophisticated air about many French shops, thanks to very attractive presentation of even the most ordinary items. You may, however, pay a bit extra for the eye appeal and for economic buying the supermarkets are first choice. Broadly speaking prices are around the same as in the UK.

There is one aspect of French shops that suits boat holidaymakers admirably: their great choice of pre-cooked dishes that can be served cold or just need heating up and help overcome any limitations in your galley. Among them are such things as *boeuf à la mode* (cold beef in jelly); various meats in many different flavoured mayonnaises; pancakes filled with meat such as turkey or chicken; many kinds of quiches; stuffed tomatoes, peppers and courgettes; and a whole host of richly-made salads. Rubbing shoulders with these will be a succulent display of *pâtés* and terrines (often freshly made locally). Not to mention all those French cheeses.

Asparagus

Where you will more than likely do your shopping, however, is in the street markets that are such a colourful feature of French towns. With so much locally-grown produce the fruit and vegetable stalls are a Technicolor glory and the cheese stalls groan under the weight of the many varieties. Whether the goods are as cheap as in UK markets is another matter, but shop like a shrewd French housewife and you'll do well. The stallholders do not bargain, though.

As you cruise along your waterway there will be plenty of opportunities to buy produce, even a chicken (certainly eggs), rabbit or fresh fish from farms and smallholdings on the banks. Some lock-keepers make a handy side-living selling such items. The one item you'll certainly find everywhere — and at a bargain price — is wine. But forget all those appel-lations, vintage years and the like. Most of the fresh local wine (often straight from the barrel) is as satisfying as any. It's good enough to travel as far as you'll cruise with it!

EATING OUT

Advice is almost unnecessary here for the choice is so great. However, a few general pointers and cautions will help. Do not expect superlative cuisine in most restaurants. You'll do best if you aim for fairly simple tasty meals, served well. Often the best spots are the unpretentious family restaurants where 'Mum' or 'Dad' does the cooking. There are plenty of these along most waterways. The larger French towns now-adays have their fair share of quick-food diners, and chips with everything (even if called *pommes frites*) is the same as in Britain.

Restaurants with umpteen rosettes in the food guides will be very, very expensive. But you can enjoy plenty of inimit-able local dishes in simpler places. There should be no prob-lem deciding before you enter anywhere since it is the law in France that eating places must display their menus outside the premises. They must also include a *table d'hôte* 'tourist menu' of a more economical price and, usually, most of them have two or three with a varying fixed charge. My recent experience is that prices compare favourably with those in the UK and are generally better value. The wines sold with meals also come more cheaply. Café owners and restaura-teurs are also more amenable to serving cheap children's portions or letting you split dishes with them.

HANDY FRENCH

Many French people not only have a reluctance to converse in English (why blame them?) but you may often find yourself in remote areas where few can speak English anyway. The following are just a few helpful phrases and words for when you really get desperate. A proper English-French guide is essential.

Common Phrases

Can you help me?	*Pouvez-vous m'aider?*
Can you direct me to …?	*Pouvez-vous m'indiquer le …?*
How far is it to …?	*A quelle distance se trouve …?*
Where can I bathe?	*Où puis-je me baigner?*
Is it safe to swim here?	*Peut-on se baigner sans danger ici?*
Where can I moor?	*Où puis-je amarrer?*
Send for a doctor	*Appelez un medecin*
Where is the nearest bank?	*Où est la banque la plus proche?*

Shopping

How much is …?	*Combien coute …?*
I want to buy	*Je voudrais acheter …*
I want more (less) than that	*J'en voudrais plus (moins) que ça*
Are these ripe (fresh)?	*Sont-ils mûrs (frais)?*

Apple	*la pomme*
Apricot	*l'abricot*
Bacon	*le lard*
Bread white (brown)	*le pain blanc (bis)*
Butter	*le beurre*
Cheese	*le fromage*
Cherries	*les cerises*
Chicken	*le poulet*
Chops	*les côtelettes*
Egg	*l'oeuf*
Fish	*le poisson*
Garlic	*l'ail*
Grape	*le raisin*
Grapefruit	*la pamplemousse*
Ham	*le jambon*
Honey	*le miel*
Jam	*la confiture*
Kidney	*le rognon*
Lamb	*l'agneau*
Lemon	*le citron*
Lettuce	*la laitue*
Liver	*le foie*
Marmalade	*la confiture d'oranges*
Milk	*le lait*
Milk shake	*le lait frappé*
Oil	*l'huile*

Onions

Onion	*l'oignon*
Pea	*le pois*
Pepper	*le poivre*
Pineapple	*l'ananas*
Raspberry	*la framboise*
Rice	*le riz*
Sausage	*la saucisse (boeuf/porc)*
Soup	*le potage*
Spinach	*les épinards*
Steak	*le bifteck*
Strawberry	*la fraise*
Sugar	*le sucre*
Veal	*le veau*

Note: A number of items with similar sounding French names have been omitted, i.e. *artichaut* for artichoke.

Eating Out

Where is a good (cheap) restaurant?	*Où y a t-il un bon restaurant (un restaurant pas cher)?*
I should like a table near the window	*Je voudrais une table près de la fenêtre*
I like it underdone (medium) (well done)	*Je l'aime saignant (à point) (bien cuit)*
May I have the bill?	*Puis-je avoir l'addition?*
Is service included?	*Le service est-il compris?*

With such a wide range of French dishes it would be hopeless trying to list them here. Most will recognise the main ingredients and those extra names usually indicate the style of cooking, e.g. *A la Marinière* for shellfish cooked in onion and white wine sauce. One of several handy food guides to France is an undoubted asset.

RECIPES

Attempting good French cuisine is something many would shun on their cookers at home, let alone in a small boat galley, but there are several simple Gallic culinary delights that you might try successfully as a fitting accompaniment for your cruise.

Crêpes

10 oz (275 g) flour
1 teaspoon salt
1 pint milk

1 tablespoon salad oil
$\frac{1}{2}$ pint ($\frac{1}{4}$ litre) water
2 eggs

Add water and milk gradually to flour, beating constantly until smooth. Add eggs, oil and salt and beat again until smooth. Leave for an hour or two.

Heat slightly greased large frying pan. To make each *crêpe* pour a serving spoon of batter into pan moving it around until surface is covered. When brown turn and cook briefly on other side. *Crêpes* should be thin.

Grated cheese (Gruyere or similar), ham or chicken cut into fine pieces can be sprinkled over *crêpes*. For sweet versions add a filling of jam, pureed pears, apricots, apples or soft fruit like strawberries with sugar. A dash of Cognac, Cointreau or Calvados adds a real French touch.

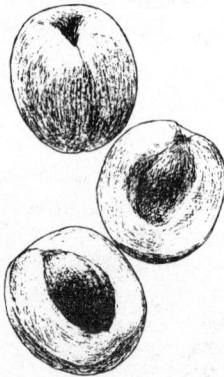

Apricots

Stuffed Brochettes

$\frac{1}{2}$ lb (250 g) slices raw
tender beef
Breadcrumbs

Chopped mixed herbs
2 cloves crushed garlic
Salt and pepper

Cut tender slices of beef about 2in wide. Make a stuffing of breadcrumbs (using about 4 slices of bread), sprinkle with oil to make a paste, add chopped mixed herbs (parsley, chives, chervil), 2 cloves of crushed garlic, salt and pepper. Mix well and press a little paste on the end of each strip of beef before rolling and threading on to a skewer. Cook for 10-15 minutes. You can use the grill or a simple barbecue (some French picnic sites have ones installed).

Bread Snacks (Pan Bagnat)

2 baguettes (long, narrow
   bread loaves) or 6 rolls
¼ pint (150ml) olive oil
4 tablespoons wine vinegar
Salt and pepper
1 garlic clove (crushed)

1lb (500g) tomatoes
1 large onion or small bunch
   spring onions
2 green peppers
1¾oz (45g) anchovy fillets
¼lb (125g) black olives

Cut loaves or rolls in half across. Sprinkle insides with a vinaigrette of olive oil seasoned with salt, pepper and crushed garlic. Lay thin sliced tomatoes, onions and peppers on bottom halves. Garnish with anchovies and olives and cover with top halves, pressing firmly together. Wrap in tin foil and place under a weight so juices can be absorbed. Serve cut into slices.

Salad Niçoise

4-5 ripe tomatoes, quartered
3 hard boiled eggs
Large tin of fish (salmon,
   tuna)

Small tin of anchovies
12 black olives
½ a red onion sliced thinly

Various other items such as a sliced pepper, artichoke hearts, lettuce heart, lightly cooked French beans, radishes and haricot beans can be added. Round off with a vinaigrette made from olive oil, chopped parsley or basil and a little crushed garlic.

Artichoke

Pêches aux Fraises

2 large peaches
¼lb (125g) strawberries (or
    raspberries)
⅓ pint (200ml) medium
    white wine

2 tablespoons red wine
5 tablespoons sugar
1oz (30g) gelatine

Peel and slice peaches and soak in white wine for 2 hours before removing. Bring wine to boil with 2 tbspns sugar and boil for two minutes. Remove from heat and add gelatine. Crush strawberries with red wine before placing in a dish with peaches on top. Add the boiled white wine as covering.

Fruit Salads

Making these looks simple but the French have developed them into a fine art. You can achieve good results by applying a few straightforward principles and a Gallic touch or two. Choose fruit with contrasting flavours and textures. Sprinkle with castor sugar to draw out the natural juices. Macerate fruits in a glass of Champagne or Cognac with a little sugar. Add a dressing made from lemon or orange juice (or both) with a little liqueur or wine added. Place whole in fridge or cold box for two hours or more (soft fruits are best added just before serving). Top off with cream flavoured with a little of the dressing. Unsalted cream cheese is used in some French fruit salads.

7

Scandinavia

Per head of population more people in this quartet of countries — Denmark, Sweden, Finland and Norway — go cruising in small boats than anywhere else in Europe. It is hardly surprising considering their great choice of routes, both inland and in well-sheltered coastal waters. What is surprising is that so few of us head north to take similar advantage of these rich opportunities for very pleasant holidays. But we are slowly finding out and more of us now cross the North Sea by several ferry routes, usually with car, and deeper across the Baltic, to go cruising.

Scandinavia certainly offers scenery that is intriguingly different and undeniably beautiful in many places. This is the land of pine forests, deep fjords, endless lakes and countless offshore islands — a world away from package crowds and concrete highrise. More than this, however, it has a cuisine and choice of foodstuffs that are refreshingly different and mostly much healthier than much of our carbohydrated, fatty dishes. Importantly, a lot of Scandinavian eating habits suit the more simple eating styles needed aboard hire craft.

A fear among many about heading north is that it is going to prove colder in summer than further south. You will soon discover, when you go, that Scandinavia can have truly hot and dry days. A clear plus enjoyed up there in the 'Land of the Midnight Sun' are the much longer hours of daylight and if you have never cruised up until late evening then this is the place to enjoy the experience. But the best time of year for a cruise holiday is from early summer or late spring until the end of August. You can get fine weather after that but days soon begin to shorten and get cold.

Each Scandinavian country has its own personality and can have quite different scenery but they all share some similarities such as their style of living. Fortunately for us, people in all these lands can often converse well in English. What unites them most, I think, is their attractive blend of traditional ways and modern methods (the farmer living in a picture-book house yet utilising the latest technology). This kind of old-world charm combined with modern business efficiency is found when hiring boats. Most hire firms there deal expertly with your bookings and maintain the craft to a high degree, which goes for the cooking equipment aboard as well.

Each land has its own peculiar style of cruising waters. These range from the massive lake network of Finland to sailing by canal across Sweden or meandering among the islands of Denmark or Norway. Wherever you go it is unlikely you will find crowded waterways — more likely just many miles with only the bountiful wildlife as company. However, you may well spend more time in the galley in some of the countries where restaurants and cafés can be a good way apart or have restricted opening times.

DENMARK

It may seem a contradiction in terms but a lot of inland cruising here is on salt water. The way in which the country has been formed out of a cluster of islands beside a broad peninsula has created a good choice of sheltered sea passages and inlets normally safe in summer for cruising. Many hardly give the impression of the sea at all. At the same time Denmark is the Scandinavian exception in that you are always close to some town or city (almost all cozily charming) in what is a more developed country than the rest. You often find yourself sailing right into the heart of some old port with the shops and eating places just a step away.

The Danish hire craft areas are primarily split between the south and east of the country around the Kattegat as it runs into the Baltic and the most northerly end in Jutland. It is this latter area that is increasingly attracting British holidaymakers in boats. Its special appeal centres around the sprawling mass of waterway known as Limfjorden that links the North Sea with the Kattegat, virtually cutting off the northern tip of the country. It is a fascinating area of scores of inlets, islands and waters both broad and narrow, many small harbours and several bigger ones like the pleasant city of Aalborg.

It is very much a go-as-you-please cruising region with more than enough choice of inlets and bays to explore in the average holiday time. And you need not have to cover the same stretch twice to get back to base. Although you are

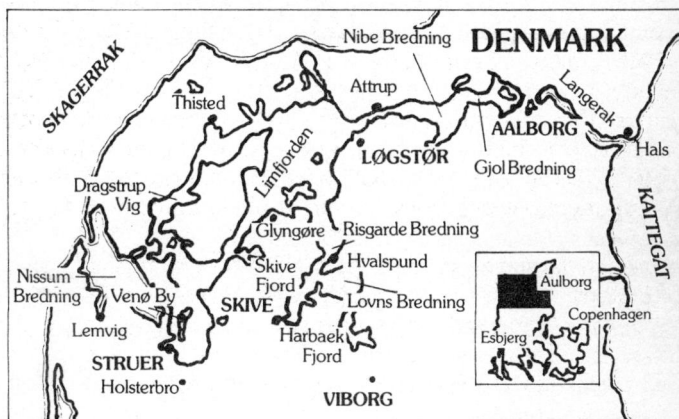

cruising in sea water there is very little tide, which eases your mooring burdens. However, since some of the reaches are pretty broad you should have one member of your party with previous boat-handling experience. You do get initial instruction before setting out and Danish craft are particularly seaworthy and well kitted out. They need to be rather more so in the south-eastern waters with their big open stretches between such major islands as Sealand and Funen. Here the skipper must have had previous open-water experience.

Whereas some of the northern routes offer wild countryside as well as the tidily manicured farms, the southern waterways can take you closer to bigger centres such as the capital Copenhagen or the Hans Christian Andersen home city of Odense. You may even begin your adventure within the shadow of Hamlet's Elsinore Castle.

Cruise Companies

Two leading British holiday boat firms offer cruises around Limfjorden:

Hoseasons Holidays, Sunway House, Lowestoft, Suffolk, NR32 3LT (tel: 0502 66622)
Blakes Holidays, Wroxham, Norwich, NR12 8DH (tel: 06053 3224)

Among a number of local Danish hire companies in Jutland are:

Dansk Badformidling, Lystbadehavnen, DK-7600 Struer (tel: (07) 87 50 55)

J.B. Marine, Elmevej 2-8, Box 20, DK-6000 Kolding (tel: (07) 85 53 64)

Limfjordens Boat Chartering II, v/John Wernberg, Syrenvej 47, Breum, DK-7870 Roslev (tel: (07) 57 61 92)

Lundboat, Kanalhavnen, DK-9670 Logstor (tel: (08) 67 25 33)

Scandinavian Boat Charter, Fasanvej 47, DK-8500 Grena (tel: (06) 32 06 57)

Hire companies in south-eastern Denmark include:

Denlice Boatcharter, Windelsvej 44, DK-5000 Odense C (tel: (09) 11 33 88)

Danish Boat Charter, Strandvejen 327, DK-2930 Klampenborg (tel: (01) 63 08 00)

Helsingor Baddudlejning, Faergevej 2, DK-3000 Elsinore (tel: (02) 21 42 55)

Holiday Charterboat, Falkonercentret, DK-2000 Frederiksberg (tel: (01) 19 09 00)

Maritim Camping, Box 26, DK-4040 Jyllinge (tel: (02) 38 83 58)

Scandinavian Boat Charter, Gadeledsvej 31, DK-3400 Hillerod (tel: (02) 25 08 38)

The Danish Tourist Board Office at 169 Regent St, London W1R 8PY (tel: 01 734 2637) can assist with further data on cruising and other information relating to the country.

Shopping

Of all the Scandinavian countries this one offers the richest and, often, most convenient scope for buying groceries. You are rarely far from shops and they are usually very well stocked. But it is common sense to buy a good supply of basics at the start of your trip so as to leave you more freedom. As elsewhere in Scandinavia shops open and close to a tight regime (usually 9a.m. to 5.30p.m. and early closing on Saturdays for the weekend). Almost all the items you get at home are on sale, even if brand names are different. You may find a lack of breakfast cereals as these are just not Scandinavian style. Surprisingly, it is not easy to find that lean Danish bacon you get at home. Cooked meats, a choice of sausages and umpteen kinds of smoked and salted fish, especially herring and eel, are available. Cheese is another good buy, and need I mention Danish pastries? Also try some of the special breads. Generally foodstuffs cost more than in the UK but their quality is as high as the hygiene in the shops.

Eating Out

The Danish, who are not backward in voicing their patriotism, boast they not only have the finest eating places in Scandinavia but also in the world. Certainly the standard is high and with greater variety than in the other three countries of the quartet. Opportunities for dining out are great, with a wide choice from first-class restaurants to many snack places. Particularly pleasant are the numerous old inns where you can either dine well or just have a light lunch. If you just want a quick bite in the park try the *smorrebrodsgudsalg* — rather a bigger mouthful than the packed sandwiches of many kinds they specialise in selling. Scandinavian open sandwiches hardly need mentioning and you will find literally hundreds of different kinds on sale.

Smorrebrod, as they are called, range from the simple (though charmingly dressed) like bread and cheese to elaborations sometimes made up of roast beef, fried egg, onions, horseradish and cucumber on black as well as white or wholemeal bread. They can be quite expensive but make a meal in themselves.

The Danes claim they invented the 'open table' but even if this is not strictly true they have perfected it to a fine art. Almost every sizeable restaurant you visit seems to have one, especially at lunchtime. Not only are they appealing to the eye but also to the pocket, as you can normally eat as much as you like for a set price. Should the children insist on chips and hamburgers Denmark, like most countries, has its spreading network of fast-food outlets.

Just a cautionary word about picnicking. The Danes can be quite fussy about where you do this. Normally they prefer you to use the special attractive sites set up for open-air meals. Be careful about parking the boat alongside a field and using it as a picnic site. Danish farmers can get angry about intrusions. And the worst crime you can commit in Denmark is to leave litter.

Note: Translations of phrases and words useful in shopping and eating out will be found on pages 75-7. Recipes are on pages 77-9.

SWEDEN

The remarkable thing about this country is that its southern portion isn't totally separated from the rest. A close look at its map shows that the large area between the capital Stockholm and the major port of Gothenburg on the opposite west coast consists largely of water. As well as two very big lakes and some smaller ones, sea inlets cut deep into the land. If these were not enough a determined aristocrat pressurised the government into creating a gigantic engineering feat linking lakes by canals and thus forging a route for ships right across the country, much of it called the Gota Canal or the 'Blue Line'.

Today this inland waterway, which took 58,000 men in 12-hour shifts 22 years to finish, is totally devoted to tourist traffic and offers cruising holidaymakers one of the finest boat trips in Europe. Its 120 miles (190km) (nearly half consisting of canals) with 58 manned locks makes a cruise in itself but there are ample opportunities for diversions and one could spend a couple of weeks just in one or two of the major lakes, Vanern and Vattern, and adjoining arms. Both lie in attractive, forested scenery and Vanern has several appealing islands on which to play Robinson Crusoe as well as a number of charming small towns around its edge.

The main canal route lies between the small port of Soderkoping on the Baltic coast and the town of Sjotorp on the eastern canal entrance into Lake Vanern. There is an extension by the Trollhatte Canal and Gota River from this lake to Gothenburg. A quarter of the way along you can make a diversion down the 50 miles (80km) of Kinda Canal to a chain of beautiful lakes. From Lake Vanern you can also head up the Dalslands Canal and lakes as far as the Norwegian border or try the Saffle Canal and its river also leading north. Bolder skippers make a round trip via Gothenburg, up sheltered coastal waters to connect with the Dalslands Canal.

The Gota Canal area can get quite busy in summer with many of the 7,000 craft that use it annually passing through but the big lakes and their tributaries do help lessen the pressure. For a more peaceful time try Lake Malaren and its connecting canals due west of Stockholm and north-east of the Gota. A good many craft are taken by Swedes with perfect calm and safety through the archipelago of islands that lead from the capital into the Baltic and down the west coast. One can also join up with the Gota from this side. Previous experience of coastal cruising is required.

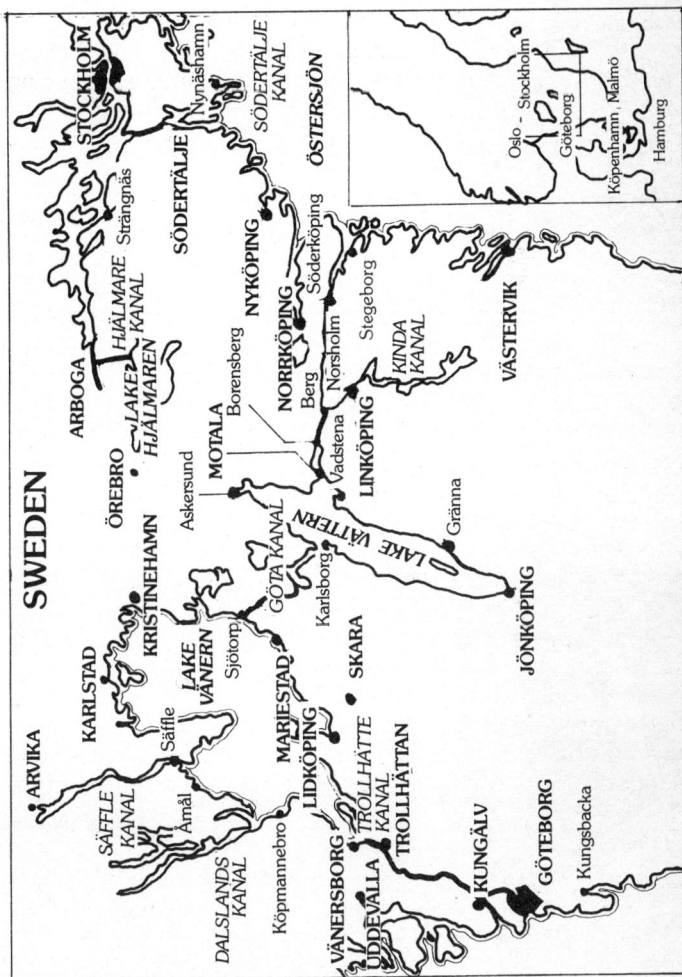

The standard of hire boats is high in Sweden and booking arrangements well handled. Having said that I must emphasise that there is a very limited number of hire firms, demand can be great, and cruisers are in short supply — so booking well ahead is essential. Among several attractive features of holidaying in these waters is the way the Swedish Touring Club (STF) operates over 400 'guest harbours' for boat tourists all around the coast and in the bigger lakes and canals. All have fresh water, toilets and facilities for refuse disposal. Some have showers and launderettes. Another appeal is that the Gota Canal offices at the two ports at each end of the system, Sjotorp and Soderkoping, will arrange to have your car driven between them to avoid you having to return the same way.

Cruise Companies

The main hire firm is Rent-A-Boat A.B., Saltsjobadsvagen 77, S-131 50 Saltsjo-Duvnas (tel: 4687 16 26 60).

The Gota Kanalbolag (Canal Co), Box 3, S-591 21 Motala (tel: 0141 535 10) can supply literature and more detailed information about hiring and waterways. For further data on Swedish inland waters contact the seemingly unlikely Swedish Forestry Commission (Domanverket) at 791 81 Falun. It owns the Gota Canal.

Useful hints on Swedish waterways are given by the National Environmental Protection Board, Box 1302, S-171 25 Solna (tel: (08) 98 18 00) in its leaflet *With Leisure Craft in Scandinavia*.

General information about the country can be obtained from the Swedish National Tourist Office, 3 Cork St, London W1X 1HA (tel: 01 437 5816).

Shopping

As in Denmark there are plenty of shops along most of your cruise routes and the Gota Canal has stores catering specially for boats. But it will pay you to take a good assortment of necessities with you if travelling out by car, for the cost of foodstuffs in Sweden can be higher than in the UK. Take tea, coffee, cereals, tinned foods and biscuits. There are, however, strict Swedish Customs limitations on the amount and types of food you can import. No fresh, frozen or smoked meat may be brought in and each visitor (over 12 years old) is restricted to 33lb (15kg), of which only 10lb (5kg) may be edible fats (butter only 5lb (2.5kg)). No more than 10lb (5kg) of fresh fruit and vegetables are allowed. Foodstuffs are also included in the maximum 600 Swedish *kronor* value of 'presents' brought in.

Some visitors think that Swedish groceries lack some variety and appetising allure but I think this is due to the exceptionally high degree of hygienic wrapping and general presentation. There is certainly a big choice available. Like Denmark you find a good array of cooked and cold items handy for serving afloat. Many foodstuffs will appeal to calorie-counters and fat-conscious eaters and one British visitor commented: 'The stores are more like health food shops'. Opening times are usually very convenient, from 9a.m. to 6p.m. weekdays and until 1p.m. Saturdays, with some super-markets staying open as late as 8p.m. (a few even open on Sundays). Many assistants speak English.

Eating Out

It is fortunate that Sweden has a good range of snack bars, cafeterias and inns serving economic meals, for its better restaurants can be really expensive. There are even Wimpys and McDondalds but there's more charm dining in country hostelries which often have that inimitable cold table of *Smorgasbord*. A local kind of fast food establishment is the *korvkiosk* selling grilled chicken and sausages, hot dogs and hamburgers — all with chips. Open sandwiches and salad dishes are a good choice in cafés. Remember that Swedes like to eat early — restaurants serve lunch from 11a.m. and country places start dinner at 6p.m. (arrive much later and you'll miss out).

You can eat more economically in restaurants if you ask for the *Dagens ratt* (meal of the day), which consists of main course, salad, soft drink and coffee. There are fixed price menus and, occasionally, eating places have 'special offers' at cut price. Try the *Husmanskost* (home cooking) based on traditional local recipes which is often served as the dish of the day. It can include pea soup with pancakes and *falukorv* (a Swedish sausage). Seafood and freshwater fish, including plenty of soused herring, prawns and smoked eel, are worth trying but can be a bit costly. One bonus is that you are usually allowed a second cup free when ordering coffee. But go easy on the wine as this is high priced and spirits such as imported Scotch and Cognac are truly expensive. The main drink in Sweden is a lager/pilsner type beer (as elsewhere in Scandinavia) and the best kind is the stronger export variety.

It pays to bring in your full quota of liquor (1 litre per person aged over 20). If you do want to buy drink for taking away in Sweden you must shop at the state-run liquor store '*Systembolaget*'.

Note: Translations of phrases and words useful in shopping and eating out will be found on pages 75-7. Recipes are on pages 77-9.

FINLAND

Some have called this Europe's forgotten country. Many ignore it under the impression that it is all pine forests (and covered in snow much of the year at that!). Yet if you joined all the water there together it would form one vast sea. At the last count there were 187,888 lakes! Many are small, of course, but the ten largest alone cover well over 4,000 sq miles (10,000 sq km). The very biggest spans 1,500 sq miles (4,380 sq km), Suur-Saimaa (Europe's fourth largest lake), which gives its end name to the country's most important lake district. The chain of lakes and connecting waterways makes this one of the best cruising regions in Europe. One of the most unspoilt and peaceful, too.

Its outstanding characteristics are the thick forests and the gently rolling countryside with small farms but it has great historic interest with ancient fortified towns, charming wooden houses and interesting old Orthodox churches. At the south-eastern edge you cruise very close to the Soviet Union. Whether you will have time to visit much of all this is another matter. The total shoreline of Suur-Saimaa, including its myriad islands, is 9,300 miles (15,000 km) — more than double that of the Caspian Sea, boast the Finns. You could have a totally escapist holiday just visiting some of the 13,710 islands and if picnicking and playing Swiss Family Robinson is your style, then this is the place for you.

For hire craft users there are two main bases — Savonlinna, with its magnificent fifteenth-century fort and centre of a famous opera festival, and Kuopio, an eighteenth-century small city and keystone to many of the lakes. I prefer Savonlinna as a place for seeing more of what's appealing in this region and it's within cruising reach of another old town worth visiting, Lappeenranta, at the lake's southern edge. By the time you have studied some of the rich wildlife, especially the water birds, and spent hours enjoying the angling, it will probably be time to turn for home.

Hire companies provide sound, well equipped craft plus the very vital charts to prevent you getting lost. You may, however, be more concerned about how to get to Finland in the first place. The best ways if going with your car are to take the ferries from the UK via Sweden or northern Germany and then on from either of those countries across the Baltic to Helsinki or a western Finnish port. It's more direct, and quicker of course, if you fly straight into the Finnish capital from Britain. The Saimaa lakes are reached by train from Helsinki.

Cruise Companies

Much of the booking is centralised in Finland. Contact the Nautic Center Oy, Karhusaari, 02100 Espoo (tel: (9) 0-455 2400) for cruising from Kuopio and Savonlinna.

Lakeland hire can also be made through Sumel Oy, Kansakoulukatu 5 B, 00100 Helsinki (tel: (9) 9-694 2044).

A number of Saimaa Lake City Tourist Offices will also advise on cruising, including those at: Imatra (Keskusasema, PB 22, 55121 (tel: (9) 54-24 666)); Kuopio (Varaskuntakatu 11, 45100 Kouvola (tel: (9) 51-296 557)); and Savonlinna (Olavinkatu 35, 57130 (tel: (9) 57-13 492)).

A few craft are available for hire for cruising among the fairly well sheltered Aland Islands and other Finnish coastal waters. Try Aland Tourist Office, Storagatan 18, 22100 Marihamn (tel: (9) 28-16 575).

The Finnish Tourist Board, 66 Haymarket, London SW1Y 4RF (tel: 01839 4048), has a good range of useful printed information.

Catering in Finland

One is almost tempted to tell summer visitors to this country to try living off the land (and water). The lakes offer up choice fish aplenty plus small crayfish, which the Finns eat by the hundreds; and the land is rich in berries of many kinds, particularly blueberries, lingonberries and the succulent cloudberries. Raspberries can grow in wild profusion in season and strawberries are easily available.

What you cannot find by yourself you can probably buy from the many small farms — including fresh eggs, chickens, vegetables and milk. They still farm in the old traditional ways in Finland, as you will tell from the tastes. One could say that much of the food produced there in all its forms is of a natural, healthily balanced kind.

Shopping

Stocking up well at the start of a cruise and at the fairly few towns you will visit is important as there could be long distances in which there is barely a house, let alone a shop. But shopping can be more of a pleasure than in some other Scandinavian lands with plenty of open-air markets as well as shops offering a good range of tempting fresh foods. Farmers and their wives bring home-grown fruit, vegetables and meats to sell from colourful stalls. Others offer fresh fish from the lakes, wild berries and those many varieties of mushrooms (try some of the forest-grown kind — they can be tastier than ordinary field mushrooms).

While you will find local grocers stocking much the same foods that you'll find elsewhere in Scandinavia the bakeries turn out a particularly fine selection of breads and cereal-based items that the Finns seems to have a flair for and treat with almost holy reverence. There is nothing better for a snack aboard or a picnic than the rye or rye and barley leaves and flatbread eaten with the flavoursome Finnish hard cheese. The country is a big producer of dairy foods, and various fish items are another good buy. And there is no shortage of meat in a country that rears 300 million tons of it.

Opening hours are usually similar to those in the UK but some places stay open later during summer when Finland also enjoys bright daylight far into the evening. Normal weekend closing is from Saturday mid-day.

Note: Government laws forbid anyone bringing more than 4lb (8kg) of tinned meat or meat products treated against infectious diseases. Dairy and egg products can only be imported on licence (this does not prevent you bringing in pasturised, heat-treated and sterilised milk, cream and egg products). Other food restrictions are similar to those in Sweden (see page 68).

Eating Out

For much of your time this could mean picnicking since restaurants and cafés are found mainly in the few towns en route and the better ones are expensive. There are, in fact, only 1,500 restaurants spread throughout Finland although there are about 4,000 cafeterias offering dishes at more reasonable prices. If you want to eat at the lowest cost try the spots named *baari (not a bar)*, *grilli*, *krouvi* or *kahvila*, although these are not licensed to sell alcoholic drinks. Also there are plenty of hamburger-type snackbars.

Smorgarsbord is just as popular here but called *voilei-papoyta* or *pitopoyta* (you'll find it easier saying the Swedish name as that language is just as easily understood here. Also, very often, is English). For hot meals try the menu-of-the-day and you should sample, once at least, the special 'Finland Menu' many places offer. A feature of most is, inevitably, reindeer in various cooking styles although, personally, I do not find it all that exciting. Finnish restaurants are classified into two grades: 'A' serving all kinds of drinks and 'B' serving just beers and wines. Mild beer is sold in cafés. Stronger Finnish beer is very good and there are some tasty vodkas and liqueurs made with local berries. Imported spirits are expensive. There are no off-licences — just the state liquor stores ('*Alko*') — but medium beers are sold in supermarkets.

While Finnish dishes can be typically Scandinavian I consider they are often more attractively presented, relying much on really fresh foods in which the flavour and goodness has been well preserved. At the same time I urge visitors not to miss the chance of joining in one of the many fresh crayfish picnics the Finns adore to hold around the lakes, usually late into the night. But beware of the constant rounds of vodka that often accompany the shellfish. The drowning rate in Finland has been abnormally high as a result.

NORWAY

If very few Britons take a hire craft holiday in Norway the reason may be that the Norwegians do not put themselves out very much to attract this kind of tourism. They have no objection to it but may have, a little too easily perhaps, accepted that their main kind of small boat cruising lacks appeal being on salt rather than freshwater. If saltwater cruising seems rather more dangerous it isn't really — not in the fine-weather summer months. Norway has a marvellous series of coastal routes very well sheltered behind the skerries (coastal islands). Include the deep fjords, well protected against Atlantic weather, and you have a very big area of safe waters.

There are a few inland boating regions such as in Telemark, southern Norway, with its two canal and lake systems linking quite a large area of beautiful mountainous and forested countryside. Many Norwegians in private craft use it but hiring boats might prove tricky. On Norway's south-eastern corner it is possible to cruise down into Sweden. Better to do so from the latter country where hire craft come more easily.

Cruise Companies

Only two of these are officially listed by the Norwegian Tourist Board as providing hire boats but local tourist offices (a list is obtainable from the Board) may be able to supply other names. The two are: Scandinavian Cruise, Seebergk-vartalet, 3200 Sandefjord (tel: 034 62296), for cruising in the large Oslo Fjord and adjoining waters; and Hardanger Jakt Sailing, P.O. Box 132, 5680 Vage-Tysnesey (tel: 054-31 100), for cruising Hardanger Fjord and surrounds.

The Norwegian Tourist Board, 20 Pall Mall, London SW1Y 5NE (tel: 01 839 6255), can supply general information about its country's coastal and inland water areas.

Shopping

Everything that applies in Sweden usually does so in Norway with shops and their contents very similar. The main difference might be that Norwegian shops, especially in the country, tend to have tighter opening times. They are also fewer and further between and you will need to be well stocked on departure from the cruise base. The cost of food-stuffs is generally high.

Eating Out

I wouldn't say that Norwegian menus are simple, for the dishes *are* attractively presented and tasty, but main courses usually consist of fairly straightforward items. Plenty of open table choice here, too, with great emphasis on fishy offerings, particularly an amazing choice of herrings in all possible forms. Better to seek out cafeterias and snack bars as restaurants can be very expensive. If you do try places with respectable menus, the smoked meats such as mutton, both hot and cold, are a speciality as is reindeer (although the radiation from Chernobyl has discouraged many from eating it in Norway). Salmon and trout in various forms from smoked to marinated are very appealing but pricey.

Norwegians provide simpler foodstuffs very well, particularly the cereal-based products. These can also be healthier and better for slimmers, such as the *Knekkebrod* (crispbread) that comes with all kinds of spreads and fillings and *Graham-*

brod, the darker loaves that most locals prefer to the white kind. Waffles (with butter or jammy spreads) are almost standard with coffee. In the sweet line try *Trollkrem* — beaten egg white and sugar with crushed cranberries, an intriguing sweet and sour flavour. You may find *Multer*, the super delicious cloudberries, on the menu although they are getting harder to find. Wines with meals are not that expensive but beer is more often drunk. Imported liquors are really costly.

HANDY SCANDINAVIAN

Three of the Scandinavian tongues, Swedish, Norwegian and Danish, have much in common although the way the Danes pronounce their language makes it seem quite different. Swedish is also one of the twin official languages of Finland. Finnish has a far different root, deriving much from Magyar, and it is unusually hard for the English to speak even when using a language guide. Therefore, to save space and prevent unnecessary repetition, only Swedish words and phrases are listed below.

Common Phrases

Good morning/afternoon/ evening	*God morgon/eftermiddag/ kväll*
How do I get to …?	*Hur kommer jag till …?*
Where is …?	*Var är …?*
I do not understand	*Jag förstar inte*
Do you speak English?	*Talar ni engelska?*
Thank you	*Tack*

Shopping

How much is it?	*Vad Kostar det?*
Baked beans	*Vita Bonor it tomat sas*
Bread, white/brown	*Franksbrod/Morkbrod*
Butter	*Smor*
Cheese	*Ost*
Chicken (frozen)	*Kyckling (fryst)*
Cod (frozen)	*Torsk (fryst)*
Coffee (ground)	*Malet kaffee*
Crispbread	*Knackebrod*
Export beer	*Starkol*
Fish fingers	*Fiskpinnar*
Fizzy drink	*Laskedryck*
Grapes	*Druvor*
Ham (smoked/boiled)	*Rokt skinka*

Lager	*Folkol*
Lamb chops	*Lambkotletter*
Milk	*Mjolk*
Mince	*Kottfars*
Onions	*Lok*
Oranges	*Apelsiner*
Pears	*Paron*
Peas tinned/frozen	*Grona artor*
Plaice (frozen)	*Rodspatta*
Plain flour	*Vetemiol*
Pork chops	*Flaskkotletter*
Prawns	*Rakor*
Sausage	*Falukorv*
Smoked salmon	*Rokt lax*
Stewing steak	*Grybitar*
Sugar	*Strosocker*
Teabags	*Thespasar*

Eating Out

Swedish restaurants offer international dishes but specialise in *nouvelle cuisine* and *husmanskost* (home-style cooking). The following includes a choice of particularly Swedish meals.

Where is there a restaurant?	*Var finns det en restaurang?*
Can I order please?	*Hur van nammet?*
Which dish do you recommend?	*Vilken rott rekomanderer ni?*
We want something simple	*Vi vill bara ha nagot enkelt*
Could I have the bill please?	*Kan jag far notan?*

Angbatsbiff	'Steamboat' steak
Attikstromming	*Stromming* pickled in vinegar
Bleak	A local white fish
Farska Potatisen	New potatoes
Gravad lax	Raw pickled salmon
Halleflundra	Halibut
Harr	Type of salmon
Isterband	Sour sausage
Kroppkakor	Potato dumplings with lingonberry jam
Kraft	Small crayfish
Laxpudding	Salmon, potato and egg
Lojrom	Bleak roe
Mandelpotatis	Tasty potato dish
Motti	Pork, lingonberries and porridge(!)

Piggvar	Turbot
Raggmunkar	A potato dish
Renkott	Reindeer
Rimmad lax	Mild cured salmon
Rokt Renstek	Smoked reindeer
Senapsgravad	*Stromming* marinated in mustard
Sill	Herring
Sjotunga	Sole
Stora	*Stromming*-like fish
Stromming	Herring-type fish
Surstromming	Fermented *Stromming*
Varmslandkorv	Beef, pork and potato sausage
Akerbar	Arctic raspberry
Brannvin	Swedish vodka
Filmjolk	Sour milk
Hjortron	Cloudberry
Jordgubbar	Strawberries
Mylta	Unsweetened berries
Ostkaka	Pastry baked with curds, cream and almonds
Spettekakan	Pastry made with many eggs
Tunnbrod	Thin cornflour bread

RECIPES

The following contain a mixture from various Scandinavian countries, mostly Danish or Finnish, as these seem to be more imaginative.

Lapland Fool

There are always leftovers when catering in a boat and this Finnish recipe makes good, easy use of them.

1½-2lb (about 4 cups) leftover meat
4 slices bacon or ham
4 cups mashed potatoes
2 bay leaves
1 dozen black peppercorns and allspice or similar
Salt
Meat stock

Chop meat into small pieces and mix with the potatoes. Add bay leaves, peppercorns, allspice and meat stock. Heat slowly while stirring constantly until mixture boils. Cover and turn off heat. Stand for around 10 minutes. Serves up to eight persons.

Cucumber Bisque

2 medium onions
3 medium cucumbers
6 tablespoons butter
2 cups of water (or chicken
  broth)

2 tablespoons flour
2 egg yolks
1/2 cup cream
Salt, pepper and parsley

Cook onions and 2 cucumbers peeled and chopped in 4 tbspns butter until onions are transparent. Add water (or broth) and cook until vegetables are tender. Press through a sieve or beat until smooth. Melt remaining butter in a pan and stir in flour until well blended. Pour in pureed vegetables and stir until smooth. Cook until thickened, stirring constantly. Beat egg yolks and cream together and stir into soup. Simmer for 5 minutes. Just before serving stir in remaining cucumber peeled and diced. Season with salt and pepper and garnish with parsley. Serves 4.

Hot Potato Salad

1 1/2 lb (750 g) new potatoes
2 oz (60 g) onion
1 1/2 oz (45 g) butter
7 1/2 fl oz (180 ml) water or
  stock

1 tablespoon wine vinegar
Pinches of sugar, salt and
  pepper
Chives or parsley

Boil potatoes in jackets before peeling and slicing. Cut onion thinly and fry in the butter until transparent. Add water or stock and simmer for 3-4 minutes. Add vinegar and seasonings. Place potatoes in this sauce to reheat. Serve garnished with chives or parsley. Cooked meats like frankfurters can be served with this dish.

Chef's Salad

1/2 Cos lettuce
Bunch of radishes
2 in (5 cm) sliced cucumber
1 onion
8 oz (250 g) cooked ham

4 oz (125 g) Danish Blue
Pinches of salt, pepper, dry
  mustard and castor sugar
4 tablespoons oil
2 tablespoons wine vinegar

Wash and cut lettuce and radishes. Slice cucumber and finely slice onion. Cut ham in fairly thick strips. Cut cheese into small cubes. Arrange all these in layers in glass bowl. In separate bowl blend seasonings with the oil gradually pouring in vinegar before pouring this dressing over the salad.

Sausage Danwich

Lettuce leaves   1 sausage
Buttered bread   1 radish
Potato salad   1 rasher crisply fried bacon

Place lettuce on bread and add as much potato salad as you like. Put sausage sliced lengthways on top. Round off with the bacon. Variations (instead of radish) can include cocktail onions, fried onions, pickles or spring onions.

Liverpâté Danwich

Lettuce leaves   Butter-fried mushrooms
Buttered bread   Gherkin
2 slices tinned or fresh pâté   Tomato slice
1 rasher of crisply fried
   bacon

Place lettuce on bread with two slices of liverpâté on top (fresh pâté can be spread direct on to bread if preferred). Add bacon and mushrooms. Place cut gherkin fanned out on slice of tomato on top.

Berry Punch

1 cup of raspberry juice or   1 cup gooseberry juice (or
   crushed and strained   tinned, strained and
   frozen raspberries (thawed)   crushed)
1 cup blackberry juice (or   2 pints (1 litre) sparkling
   frozen kind similarly   water
   treated)   2 pints (1 litre) lemon soda
                          ice

Combine the juices, cover and place in fridge or ice box for some hours. Just before serving pour in sparkling water and soda. Serve over ice cubes in punch bowl or glasses.

8
Holland

Think of canals and you think of Holland. But that is about all most people consider about inland waterways in this flattest of all European lands. Yet there are many miles of natural rivers and lakes as well. When it comes to hire craft cruising you could also add a stretch of the North Sea coast protected by islands. All in all there are 4,600 miles (7,400 km) of the inland kind and covering a richer variety of scene and sightseeing interest than most people imagine.

With such a good choice it is obviously important to pay close attention to which area you choose for your holiday. Just as vital is selecting the type of waterways to best suit you and your crew. Many of the canals carry heavy commercial traffic and some of those barges are as big as many a sea-going ship. But there are a lot of smaller, quieter routes that may carry some commercial craft but are reasonably easy for motor cruiser handling. Some canals and rivers are exclusive to holiday craft.

The region that British tour operators choose most for their cruise packages is Friesland, that large area north of Amsterdam, and bordering the massive Ijsselmeer artificial lake, that is Holland's dairy produce larder. Here you sail between lush green fields on which the famous Friesian cows graze to produce Dutch cheeses and butter. Tulips and other flowers are also grown here while hundreds of windmills turn slowly. Apart from the scenic joys a particular advantage is that locks are few and far between. There are plenty of bridges, but these are quickly opened for you by the keepers as you have the right of way over road traffic.

Cruising through a fine network of canals you pass a succession of small villages and busy little towns (mooring right in their centres close to shops and restaurants). There is Makkum where they make Delft-like blue china; charming

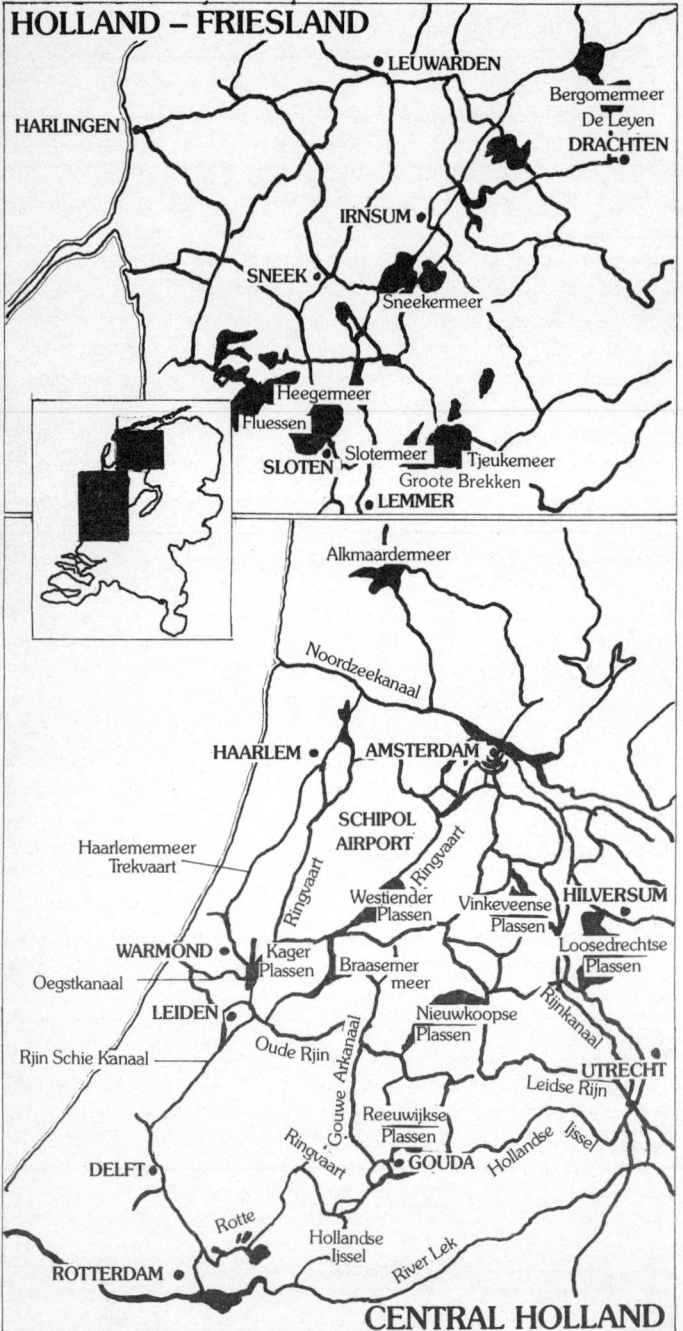

HOLLAND – FRIESLAND

LEUWARDEN

HARLINGEN

Bergomermeer
De Leyen
DRACHTEN

IRNSUM

SNEEK

Sneekermeer

Heegermeer

Fluessen

SLOTEN

Slotermeer

Groote Brekken

Tjeukemeer

LEMMER

Alkmaardermeer

Noordzeekanaal

HAARLEM

AMSTERDAM

SCHIPOL
AIRPORT

Haarlemmermeer
Trekvaart

Ringvaart

Ringvaart

Westiender
Plassen

Vinkeveense
Plassen

HILVERSUM

WARMOND

Kager
Plassen

Braasemer
meer

Loosedrechtse
Plassen

Oegstkanaal

LEIDEN

Nieuwkoopse
Plassen

Rijnkanaal

Rjin Schie Kanaal

Oude Rjin

UTRECHT

Leidse Rijn

Gouwe Arkanaal

Reeuwijkse
Plassen

Hollandse Ijssel

DELFT

Ringvaart

GOUDA

Hollandse
Ijssel

River Lek

Rotte

ROTTERDAM

CENTRAL HOLLAND

Sneek (to bely its name); equally appealing Leeuwarden, the region's capital; and Joure, where they make the well-known Friesland clocks.

Another popular area for British cruising fans is south Holland, on the other side of Amsterdam, a region with an equally complex chain of waterways. Here you can mix canals with rivers and lakes and even go very close to seaside resorts like the major one of Scheveningen. The many routes take you into the centre of some of Holland's most interesting old cities and towns, including Leiden with the country's oldest university, Delft, the home of the world famous china and The Hague, the seat of government. In springtime no one wants to miss the beautiful flower exhibition grounds at Keukenhof. The canals can carry you right into the centre of Amsterdam itself.

Given time and determination there is no reason why you cannot cruise right into north Holland, visiting the cheese town of Alkmaar and the old Zuider Zee ports. Those who want to hire craft from local boat firms can explore a lot more of Holland, including Zeeland further south — virtually a set of islands linked by bridges, dams and canals. You might still spot some inhabitants in traditional Dutch costume and clogs. Further east you can cruise up to West Germany.

Paradoxically a big attraction of this country is the ease with which boat hirers can tour inland away from their craft. Being so flat it is admirable for cycling, and some hire cruisers come with bicycles aboard. (No problem hiring if these are not provided.) The standard of boats is good and some very similar types to the ones in the UK from the streamlined to those with elongated cabins, are available. There is no difficulty finding mooring places and these are almost always free. Having lived from and on the water so long many Dutch people pay particular attention to your needs and the hire organising is excellent.

Holland may look small on the map but do not attempt to cruise more than a small portion of it. Boats are strictly limited by law to a speed of only 6 miles (10 km) per hour on narrow canals and rivers or 12 miles (20 km) on broader water (on some lakes these speed restrictions are lifted). On the very big waterways like the Rhine, international navigation rules apply. Hire companies will advise you of these.

CRUISE COMPANIES

There are nearly 50 hire firms spread around Holland, too many to list here but full details of them, their craft and charges, can be found in a very useful brochure issued by the Netherlands Board of Tourism and entitled *Holland Watersports Paradise*. It is available from the Board's office at 25 Buckingham Gate, London SW1E 6LD (tel: 01 630 0451). Many Britons book their cruise holiday through UK tour operators, the two leading companies being:

Hoseasons Holidays, Sunway House, Lowestoft, Suffolk NR32 3LT (tel: 0502 66622)
Blakes Holidays, Wroxham, Norwich NR12 8DH (tel: 06053 3224)

These firms will also arrange ferry bookings for yourselves and car to Holland.

'VVV', the official tourism organisation within Holland, has also arranged a special hire cruise package with one of the country's leading boat operator's in the Friesland area. For this you can contact Friesland Boating, De Tille 5, 8723 ER Koudum (tel: 05142-2607).

For greater detail on the country itself apply to the Netherland Board of Tourism (address above).

SHOPPING

There could hardly be an easier cruise country for shopping than this one. Often you tie up right outside a grocery or supermarket. Shopping hours are much the same as in the UK. Many of the items carried in the shops will be familiar to you — even as far as the brand names. There is hardly any need to take much with you in the car but some cereals, marmalades and brands of tea could be worth carrying over. You would also save some money doing some pre-cruise shopping in the UK as Dutch prices tend to be a little higher (allowing for the exchange rate). A number of waterway boat centres have shops selling basic items. You may even come across a shop on a boat!

EATING OUT

It may be a sign of how international Dutch restaurants have become that nowadays they have to put a special symbol outside those that still offer traditional-style dishes. Called the *Neerlands Dis* it takes the form of a red, white and blue soup tureen. The symbol may also underline the fact that the natives are hot on soups. But if you want to get away from

the typical food you find as common in Holland as at home
— including fast food outlets — then try these places that are
full of old Dutch décor, panelled and cozy. The meals can
include such items as asparagus with ham, brown beans with
bacon and eel stew — tastier than they may sound. Like a
lot of Dutch traditional dishes they can be heavy in
calories — for example *boerenmeisjes* (farmgirl's pudding and
cream).

It is claimed that in the bigger Dutch cities you can now
eat in almost 'any language', although Indonesian seems to
be the more prominent foreign tongue. Imported many
decades ago from the Dutch East Indies, as it then was,
Rijstafel (rice table) type meals are very common but they
can contain up to 50 separate dishes and you might be wiser
asking for the *Nasi Goreng*, a smaller variety. But keep such
dining out for more special occasions as it can be expensive.
Better to seek out the restaurants displaying the blue tourist
menu sign where you can get a starter, main dish and dessert
for around £5-£6. A leaflet giving names and addresses of
these eating places is obtainable from local tourist offices or
from the Netherlands Board of Tourism in London (for
address see page 84).

Almost everywhere you cruise you will find that Dutch
institution — the café — much more a meeting place than in
Britain, and ranging from those in the busy city-centres full of
younsters to what is barely more than someone's living room
with a few old-timers sitting around. Try also the Dutch
version of a pub or *bruine kroeg* (brown pub), usually simple
and more like a café than a bar. Not surprisingly there are
some floating restaurants scattered around the vast waterway
system.

HANDY DUTCH

You should have very little problem in Holland finding someone who speaks English. It is almost the second tongue
throughout the country and local disc jockeys seem to speak
it as much as their own language! Hopefully, though, you
may cruise in truly rural areas where the way of life has
remained typically Dutch to the point of remaining mono-
lingual. If so then the following could help:

Common Phrases

Is this the right way to …?	*Gaat deze weg naar …?*
Where can I find …?	*Waar is …?*
Do you speak English?	*Spreekt er iemand Engels?*

How far is it from here to …?	*Hoe ver is het van hier naar …?*
Which is the way to the bulbfield?	*Hoe kom ik op het bij de bollenfelde?*

Shopping

Where is the …	*Waar is …?*
… baker?	*… de bakker?*
… butcher?	*… de slager?*
… dairy	*… de melkboer?*
… fishmonger?	*… de visboer?*
… grocer?	*… de kruidenier?*
… greengrocer?	*… de groetenboer?*
I want to buy …?	*Ik wil graag …?*
How much is it?	*Hoeveel kost het bij?*

Bacon	*het spek*
Beef	*het rundvlees*
Bread	*het brood*
Cake	*het taartje*
Carrots	*de worteljes*
Cauliflower	*de bloemkool*
Cheese	*de kaas*
Chicken	*de kip*
Chops	*de carbonade*
Cream	*de room*
Egg	*het ei*
Kidney	*de nier*
Lamb	*het lamsvlees*
Lemon	*de citroen*
Lettuce	*de sla*
Meat	*het vlees*
Oil (corn)	*de slaolie*
Oil (olive)	*de olijfolie*
Orange	*de sinaasappel*
Peas	*de erwten*
Pie	*de pastei*
Pork	*het varkensvlees*
Potatoes	*de aardappelen*
Raspberry	*de framboos*
Salad cream	*de slasaus*
Salt	*het zout*
Sausage	*de worst*
Strawberries	*de aardbeien*
Veal	*het kalsvlees*
Vinegar	*de azijn*

Note: A good many Dutch food names have much the same sound as English, especially for drinks, so if some are not listed above just try your normal word.

Eating Out

Where can we eat?	*Waar kunnen we eten?*
At what time is dinner served?	*Hoe laat is het diner?*
We only want a snack	*Wij willen maar een hapje*
Which dish do you recommend?	*Welk gerecht kunt U ons aanbevelen?*
I like it underdone/medium/ well done	*Ik wil het graag rauw/half doorgebakken/goed doorgebakken*
The bill, please	*Mag ik de rekening?*

Apart from the fact nearly all Dutch eating places have menus in English even the ones in Dutch have many dishes fairly easily understood. The following are just some of the more specific Dutch dishes:

Bitter Ballen	Meat balls with mustard
Blinde Vinken	Stuffed meat rissoles
Bloemkool met Spek	Cauliflower and bacon
Bruine Bonen met Spek	Brown beans with salt bacon
Ertwensoep	Thick pea soup with smoked sausage
Groetensoep	Clear soup with meat balls
Hachee	Beef and onion stew
Hutspot met Klepstuk	Beef, vegetables and milk
Jachtschotel	Meat, vegetable and apple stew
Paling	Smoked eels on toast
Rolpens met Rodekool	Minced beef and tripe
Stokvis Schotel	Cod and rice with onions, potatoes
Uitsmijter	Cold meat, fried egg on bread
Suurkool met Worst	Smoked sausage and cabbage
Haagse Bluff	A whipped dessert
Pannakoeken	Sweet or savoury pancakes
Pojfertjes	Fritters
Wafels me Slagroom	Waffles and cream

Beer is the standard drink and although wines are readily available they can be costly. *Genever* (gin) is drunk with everything.

RECIPES

Much traditional Dutch cooking is on the heavy side, often needing plenty of stove time and therefore unsuitable for catering in hire craft. However, if you don't mind having the pot on the boil for several hours, there are some tasty stews. I've chosen a mix of both quicker and slower dishes reasonably simple to prepare.

Hete Bliksem (Hot as lightning)

4lb (2kg) potatoes	Salt, butter, pepper
1½lb (¾kg) eating apples	16 rashers bacon
2lb (1kg) cooking apples	

This is to serve six hearty Dutch eaters so you may want to have less of each ingredient. Cut peeled potatoes into even sized pieces. Quarter apples after coring and peeling. Place potatoes and apples into saucepan with salt and water and bring to the boil, simmering gently for 30 minutes, covered. Drain and mash with butter and pepper to taste. Keep warm on serving dish in oven while you fry bacon until crisp. Lay rashers on top of the mash.

Boerenkool met Worst (Kale and Cabbage)

3lb (1½kg) curly kale or cabbage	2oz (50g) butter
	Milk
3lb (1½kg) potatoes	Pepper (best fresh ground)
1lb (500g) smoked sausage or frankfurters	

This is really a winter dish but Holland, like Britain, can have some cold, wet summer days. Shred kale or cabbage finely and simmer for up to 40 minutes in lightly salted boiling water. Add peeled, quartered potatoes, sausage and remaining water. Boil gently for 30 minutes until potatoes are done. Remove sausage and mash potatoes and greens with butter and milk to make a purée. Season with pepper, place on serving dish with sausages on top.

Bruine Bonen met Spek (Brown Beans with Bacon)

1lb (500g) brown beans	Salt
3 large onions	
¾lb (350g) streaky bacon (in one piece)	

Wash beans, cover with water and soak overnight. Boil for 1-2 hours in the same water adding a level teaspoon salt when beans are half cooked. Peel and slice onions and cube the bacon. Fry the bacon in its own fat until crisp, golden brown. Fry onions in bacon fat and after draining beans serve the whole together.

To achieve the real Dutch result, if you have the stomach and a sweet enough tooth, you make a sauce by gently heating ½lb (250g) of molasses or black treacle with a knob of butter and serve it over the dish piping hot!

Leidse Hutspot (Leiden Hotpot)

2lb (1kg) lean beef (flank or topside)
2lb (1kg) carrots
2lb (1kg) onions
2lb (1kg) potatoes
Salt and pepper

Cover beef in large pan with water. Bring to boil and skim surface. Cover pan and simmer for three hours until tender. Remove from pan and keep hot in oven, reserving beef stock. Peel and slice vegetables into moderate-sized even pieces. Place them in clean pan and half cover with stock. Bring to boil, cover and simmer for 20 minutes or until vegetables are cooked but not soft. Mash with small amount of stock and add salt and pepper to taste. Carve boiled meat into thin slices, pile mashed vegetables on a warm dish and arrange meat on top. This serves up to six and you may prefer smaller amounts.

Snacks

Although the Dutch do not go in for the *Smorgasbord* type of eating as much as the Scandinavians, they have plenty of the ingredients with which you can make something similar. Some of the cheeses are well known, like Gouda and Edam, but also try the Leyden, firmer and yellower and often flavoured with caraway seeds and pepper. You will also find that cheeses sold in Holland can be more mature than those on sale in the UK. Also try the herring, shrimp and eel appetisers.

9
Faraway Waterways

If cruising Europe's canals and rivers can prove the most relaxing holiday you have ever had then doing so along some of the fascinating waterways in more distant parts of the globe can be the adventure of a lifetime. Can you imagine following the trail of those old gold panners in California or of sailing across Ned Kelly country in Australia? Canada's wilder 'Mountie' country is another possibility — and there are scores of similar opportunities.

One drawback, of course, is finding enough holiday money for your faraway flight. However, once you are in your chosen floating adventure playground the cost is little more than in the UK. There are plenty of well organised hire craft operations in the USA, Canada and Australia, and if you are already planning to make a long-haul trip then it is worth considering including a waterway cruise in your itinerary.

Self-catering afloat in these countries is not as difficult as you might have assumed from the remoteness of some of the regions. In the States, for example, operators will even stock up your craft for the whole of your holiday so you need never buy a thing. In any event none of the waterways mentioned are that far from civilisation and there is usually a town close by where shopping is possible. Parts of Canada may be the exception and there the boat firms also ensure you have plenty of supplies. In all these regions fishing is usually excellent so you can always land your supper. In Australia and parts of America local authorities often provide special picnic areas (with barbecues) along popular cruise routes, mainly to ensure you don't set a forest fire going, but it's a relaxed way of dining out. Proper restaurants or fast-food outlets always

91

seem round the next bend in the USA and Australian water-ways almost always have some eating spot along your daily route.

USA

If you believe Arizona is all Badlands, Kentucky just 'Green Grass' country, and Tennessee only a jazz centre then think again. They all offer very good chances to enjoy fine lake and river cruising. In fact all over the States you can find similar opportunities. Many waterways are broader and far longer than in Europe but they are not all as long as the Mississippi and there are plenty of them where you can idle along with-out worrying about the navigation. Many take you closer to wildlife and virgin territory than those you can find this side of the Atlantic. In such a big country, of course, there can be great differences in climate and you may prefer more temper-ate regions like those of the northern States or hot areas such as cruising the Sacramento River in California (a par-ticularly outstanding trip). Florida, another warm territory, has some intriguing waters to follow.

Almost everywhere there is good angling and this can even include sea fishing. One of the outstanding routes lies along a large length of the US east coast — the Intra-Coastal Water-way — inside several chains of islands close inshore. It can take you close to big northern cities or into the real sub-tropical 'Deep South' of the Carolinas and Florida. Elsewhere you can cruise around extensive lake districts.

One difference between US and European hire craft is that the US variety are often more like mobile houseboats — blunt-ended and square. But this means you have more comfortable living aboard, including good galleys. Many also have outboards rather than inboard engines (ensuring more living room), but these still give you a good speed. Just as simple to handle as those in Europe, you should find no problem adapting to US-type craft. Indeed a growing number of Europeans are already enjoying the American waterways.

At the time of writing there are no package deals available that include air travel and the hire boat, which means you will have to arrange your own transport and bookings. For economy take advantage of the cheaper flights that are often advertised (usually on an advance booking basis). There are now direct services from the UK to major airports within reasonable reach of many of the cruising areas. Consult your travel agent. For more details of waterways and hire compan-ies contact the US Travel and Tourism Office, 22 Sackville St,

London W1X 2EA (tel: 01 439 7433). A useful book is *Adventure Trip Guide*, published by Adventure Guides Inc, 36 East St, New York, NY 10022.

CANADA

Think of this country and you immediately think of its Great Lakes — but not of its many other waterways. Yet there are innumerable ones where you can hire a cruiser for a more idyllic, relaxing trip than battling with the sometimes rough waters of those massive inland seas called the Great Lakes. The majority of organised boat holidays are in Ontario Province or thereabouts. And these include not just trips on rivers and lakes but on some lengthy canals such as the Rideau Waterway which connects Ottawa with Kingston.

Other popular routes include the Trent Severn Waterway, a 239 mile (385 km) link between Trenton on Lake Ontario with Port Severn in Georgian Bay off Lake Huron. Georgian Bay is also a big area for cruising. You can also follow the big ship route through parts of the vast Great Lakes system but you might prefer the calmer waters of a detached area called Lake of the Woods, although it is not all that much smaller — a 65,000 mile (110,000 km) shoreline and 14,000 islands. You can really get away from it all on the lakes and rivers of Canada with moose and beavers far more common than people.

Further information is available from the Canadian Tourist Office, Canada House, Trafalgar Sq, London SW1Y 5BJ (tel: 01 629 9492). Ask for a useful guide called *Boating*, which features the Ontario region.

AUSTRALIA

If this continent was not so very far away from the more populated Western countries its rich choice of rivers and lakes would have made it one of the most popular cruising destinations anywhere. Even so the Aussies have not wasted the great opportunity to develop several waterways for hire boating. Mainly in the states of Victoria, South Australia and New South Wales they offer a variety of scenery, route and type of craft. You can cruise through national parks packed with wildlife (including lots of kangaroos) or even make a trip close to a magnificent ocean beach. And if you have never operated a paddle boat you will have the chance on the Murray and Darling Rivers and elsewhere. These mini-paddlers (more like big houseboats) prove more economical and less susceptible to damage from river obstructions.

Perhaps the most popular waters are the Gippsland Lanes, Australia's biggest inland waterway that lies close to the famous Ninety Mile beach (separated by a sand dune) not far from Melbourne. The scenery here is not too unlike that seen in parts of rural England although it is very different if you hire a craft on another major set of lakes, the Eildon system, also in Victoria, situated in bushland.

Facts about hire companies and regions are obtainable from the Australian Tourist Commission, 20 Savile Row, London W1X 1AE (tel: 01 434 4371).

PART III
SELF-CATERING AT SEA

10

Introduction

Not long ago the need for a handy guide to self-catering at sea would have been fairly limited. Most Britons pushing the boat out on the seas and oceans were a pretty experienced lot with a reasonable knowledge of how to store their craft and could probably cook a decent meal in a force 8 gale. But in recent years there has been a remarkable change with many people with very limited experience of yachting — or even none at all — spending their holidays hauling on spinnakers, sheets and other assorted nautical gear. Their notions of catering in a seagoing craft are, possibly, just as inexperienced.

The chief reason for this fast-growing trend is the introduction of what is called 'flotilla sailing' — the organising of small fleets of easy-to-handle yachts, usually numbering six to eight in all, under the careful supervision of professional yachtsmen in a mother craft. Safer, more sheltered seas, such as the Adriatic, Ionian and parts of the Aegean/Mediterranean, are chosen where there are plenty of handy islands and coastal inlets. Yachts usually follow a set route, although the more capable skippers are allowed to wander off alone before the fleet normally meets up again for the night.

Flotilla holidays are sold in the UK by around a dozen specialist companies, usually with plenty of experience in hiring out yachts. Their package deals include the return air travel; the instructions given by the professionals; plenty of useful printed advice; and some holiday fun such as barbecues and drinks parties. A few also offer short, say three- or four-day, pre-cruising courses at a British or foreign base for anyone needing experience in yacht handling. Basically all that these firms demand is that the skipper alone must have had experience of handling boats under sail, although in some cases this need only have been in dinghies. The 'crews',

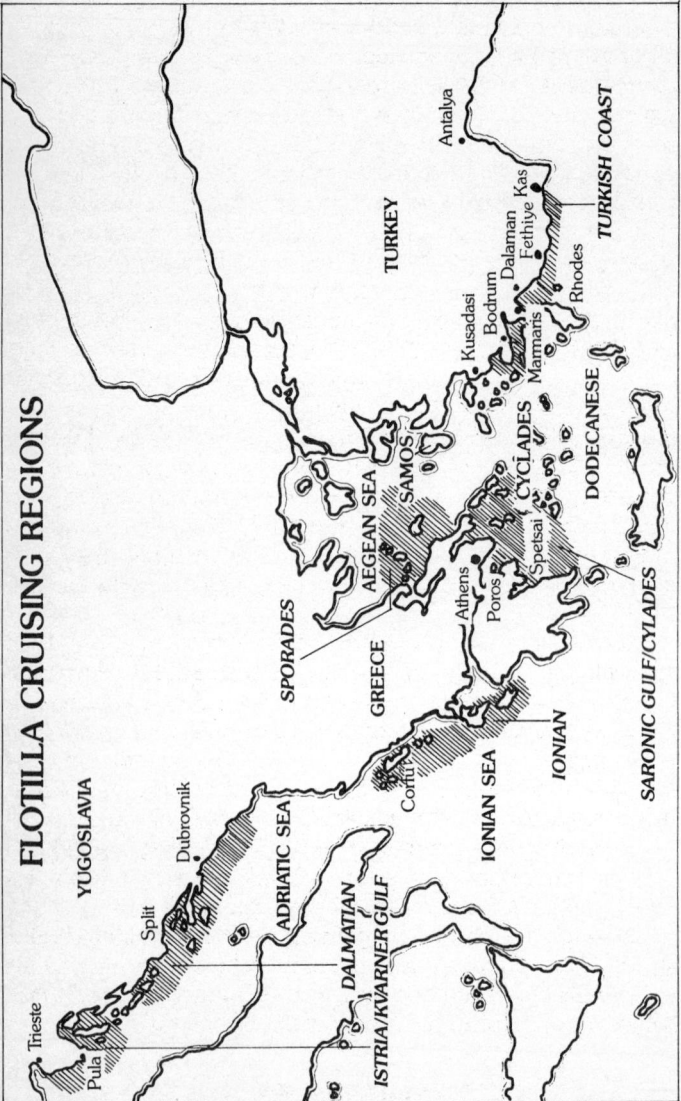

FLOTILLA CRUISING REGIONS

often rank landlubbers, usually adapt very quickly to the simple maritime skills needed, children frequently proving the most capable.

The secret of flotilla holiday success is that the companies have shown great forethought in the selection of their types of yacht. Ranging in size from around 25 feet to just over 40 (8-11m) (about 32-36 feet (10-11m) is common), with comparatively small sail areas (330 square feet of canvas is typical), they also have easy-to-handle gear. Thanks to roller-reefing and conveniently placed halyard winches, sails can be controlled directly by the skipper from the cockpit. There are usually just the two sails: mainsail and foresail — designed so that the yachts can usually be sailed as fast or as slow as skippers feel capable of going (given the right wind).

If there is no wind, or too much for comfort, there is always the small engine with its simple controls. Should craft still get into trouble, relief in the form of the 'mother ship' can arrive fairly quickly by use of the VHF radio on its set frequencies. This is also a useful way of ensuring one does not get lost. However, according to the boat firms, mishaps are few and far between, including the danger most new-comers to yachting fear most — falling overboard. Although initially it is easy enough to trip up on the running gear and other ropes, or to get hit by the boom, people appear to adapt quickly and soon find their sea sense as well as their sea legs.

It can be surprising, too, how speedily most adapt to using the really small galley and cooking equipment found in these yachts, which are even smaller than in most inland waterway boats and usually consist of no more than a two-ring stove with small oven, an ice box as a fridge and cramped storage space. It is hardly surprising that some chicken out and eat as many meals ashore as they can, but this isn't always possible when moored or anchored in some isolated bay and, in any case, as I shall show further on it is possible to turn out some appetising, interesting dishes without too much fuss.

Although this part of the guide is mainly devoted to flotilla sailing it can equally apply to many others who hire yachts independently. There are also, if much more limited, possi-bilities for sea cruising in motor craft without sail.

YOUR BOAT

In selecting craft that are reasonably easy to sail the holiday boat firms have mostly chosen types of a fairly similar design where the main variations, both inside and out, are size. That these yachts have to have curved hulls and reasonably pointed bows to aid sailing qualities means they must be more cramped than boats on rivers and canals. They often have less headroom as well. Given all this they can still be reasonably comfortable and the hirers have done their best to provide as many conveniences as possible. But I would advise you put your ability to handle a yacht before seeking a bigger one with more room. Size should depend on the amount of crew.

A typical layout inside working from fore to aft includes a small cabin in the bows with a pair of single berths (occasionally a double bunk). Shaped to the hull it is the most cramped part of the yacht and can best suit small children. This cabin is normally followed by separate washbasin and lavatory on each side, usually with a shower fitting (and electric razor socket). Loos can be electrically flushed or, often, hand pumped. Amidships is the saloon with benches on either side that seat a minimum of four and can be converted into berths for one person each. A collapsible table is provided for meals. Headroom is better here thanks to the raised cabin deckhead that normally stands 6 ft (1.8m) high. Opening out from the saloon is the tiny galley with small cooker, sink and ice box (a few yachts do have an electric fridge). Opposite can be found a cupboard for hanging clothes. Right aft, approached by steps leading under the cockpit, is the main sleeping cabin with two single or one double berth (a few have one single and a double).

Out of sight are freshwater tanks with enough supplies for two or three days if used carefully. In most ports topping up is made through pipe connection to quayside taps. You save freshwater if you wash up in salt water and just rinse in fresh. Most yachts also have a sewage tank to prevent polluting the sea. Stowage space for clothes and food is found under berths and in nooks and crannies.

The cockpit with its navigational instrumentation, wheel, chart table and engine controls has also to serve as the main sunbathing area since open deck space is very limited and at sea you do not want to get entangled with the rigging. It is important, therefore, to try and choose a type of craft that offers as much cockpit room as possible for the number aboard. Skippers never take kindly to having suntan lotion and coffee spilled over charts. Sitting on a pair of dividers can give added point to this. Neatness aboard is a priority so coil up those lines and ropes tidily to avoid tripping up on them. A lifeline that can be clipped to some standing part or rigging is a wise precaution if very young children are aboard

4-Berth Yacht. Ideal for the less experienced.

Length overall 27ft.;
beam 9ft.;
draught 4ft.;
461 sq.ft. sail;
10 h.p. engine.

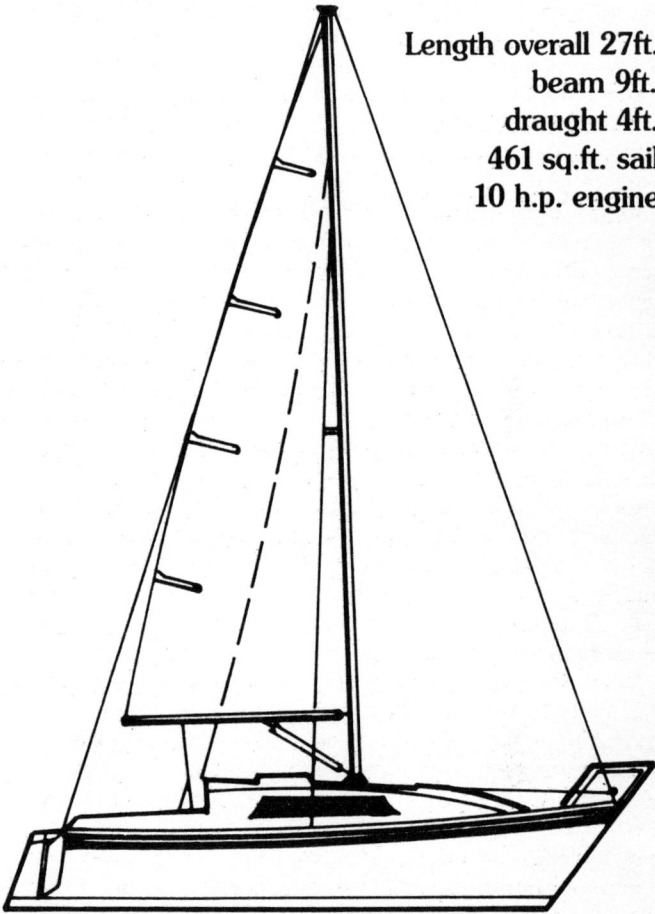

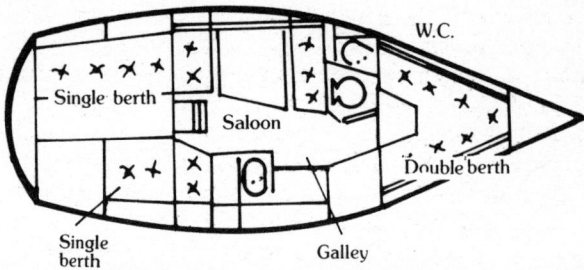

W.C.

Single berth

Saloon

Double berth

Single
berth

Galley

so check with the company to see if it can be provided or get your own. Lifejackets for all are standard equipment and you should also make sure that ones suitable for youngsters are provided if necessary.

Additional items often provided aboard can include a rubber dinghy — essential for getting to and from yachts at anchor and handy for fishing trips. A few companies provide fishing lines but you may have to take your own. Fish can be a useful part of your diet. Some hirers provide snorkels and flippers aboard as all the waters in which the flotillas operate are beautifully clear for underwater sightseeing. A boarding ladder, highly useful when swimming over the side, and a sun awning are standard equipment. Instruments for chart plotting are also provided but it pays to take your own binoculars since everyone will want to see where they are heading.

11

Seawise Ways

BOAT HANDLING

Skippers must have some previous sailing experience, even if it is limited to dinghies, and it is important not to cheat on this As safe as flotilla yachting has proved you will enjoy your floating holiday all the more knowing you have the confidence to handle most problems. An obvious lack of experience will certainly unnerve your crew. It is best to take the pre-holiday courses offered by some companies. The professionals on the spot give you a good teach-in before you set sail and will keep a special eye on anyone displaying a lack of confidence and ability. Many people taking these trips join together to share their previous experience and also the skippering and I think this is both the wisest and most relaxing way of doing it. But in the confines of a small boat you need to know your companions well.

CLOTHING

What you wear on the open seas is much more important than clothing needed on an inland waterways holiday. Yachts just do not have the space for anything but sheer essentials. Forget jackets or that extra pair of trousers. Stick to the most casual clothes you've got — a pair of slacks, shorts, sports shirts or T-shirts, change of underwear and the lightest and least crushable of clothing. A warm jumper to wear for cooler evenings on deck or if there is a sharpish wind blowing is a useful addition. Special attention should be paid to shoes, which must be of the non-slip kind for use on wet decks or for clambering over rocks ashore. See that they are sturdy, too. A reasonably waterproof anorak is helpful when sitting in the cockpit in the rain. If you are subject to sunburn more than most wear long-sleeved items and also a broad-brimmed hat (you are exposed more and for longer when in a boat). For handling the anchor and cable a pair of tough gloves is useful.

WASHING

With freshwater aboard limited you may choose to have a shower or a bath ashore. A number of yacht marinas provide shower facilities in toilet blocks. Some include washing sinks for doing your laundry.

LUGGAGE

The type as much as the lack of baggage is important. There is nowhere aboard to stow suitcases so it is recommended you carry your gear in what are called 'sailing bags'. Made from strong PVC-coated nylon and with webbing handles they are soft enough to be squeezed in a drawer or cupboard bottom while still proving roomy enough to take a surprising amount of clothing. But ensure you do not put in breakables — airport baggage handlers are not that gentle.

SWIMMING

A good deal of your time will be spent swimming over the side as well as from beaches. It is vital, therefore, that you observe great care, especially where children are concerned. It is wisest to take some form of inflatable safety fitting for youngsters and adults should not feel ashamed to wear something similar if they are indifferent swimmers. Always have someone on watch while anyone is in the water while at anchor; make sure the boarding ladder is in place and have the yacht's dinghy standing by

FISHING

I have seen amateur yachtsmen towing a line behind them while their craft is underway but you are unlikely to catch much this way. Neither will you land anything worthwhile at anchor in shallower bays. Best to reef in sail and drift along for a while out at sea or take the dinghy and fish from that. An ordinary hand-held line will probably catch as much as an expensive rod. The easiest and best way is to come up alongside some local commercial fishing boat and buy your fish. A less smelly way of cooking the catch than in the tiny galley is to make a temporary barbecue on some deserted beach where there is plenty of driftwood.

ENTERTAINMENT

On most flotilla cruises you always call in at some livelier as well as smaller harbours and there is usually a disco or even a night club around. The holiday company also arranges two or three fun evenings such as a 'pirates party' and with several other yacht crews always around there is no shortage of company for your own shindig.

HEALTH

You are going to spend a lot of time many miles and hours away from the nearest doctor or chemist so take any medicines and other treatments for health problems you feel you and your crew might be subject to in particular. Among basic medications you should also include pain-killers, digestive aids, sunburn lotion, antihistamine ointment and Alka-Seltza (you'll drink a lot of wine). A first-aid box should be on board but take some plasters, scissors and a fine needle for removing splinters. Yes, do take sea-sick treatments, although I doubt if you'll run into much rough weather on most routes.

INSURANCE

All the yacht companies offer some form of travel insurance covering the usual risks for health and loss and including cancellation of your trip. But check to see cover is adequate for all the risks you are likely to face, including yacht damage in full. Many policies do not cover water-skiing and sub-aqua diving except on payment of an extra premium.

LAUNDRY/BEDDING/TOWELS

You will start your cruise with fresh laundered bedsheets and pillow slips but you will have to wash them yourselves or try and find a launderette ashore when you need to launder them or other items again. Detergents are provided aboard. Blankets are provided but in most warm sea regions these may not be necessary. You should take your own towels, including ones for the beach.

SHOREGOING

The yacht firms normally select routes that offer a variety of ports of call, ranging from busy harbours to deserted coves. A good itinerary should include a star port with plenty of sightseeing interest; a couple of smaller ones where you can see local life at its simple, more charming best; and several isolated bays or inlets that add to the sense of adventure and escapism. Avoid routes with too many package resorts and crowds as that's what most want to avoid by going sailing. You'll do a lot of walking ashore to stretch your legs so take sturdy footwear. Rucksacks are a useful asset.

12

Cooking at Sea

There are two distinct schools of thought about preparing meals on holiday yachts. One insists: 'Don't! Eat ashore.' The other, more boldly, states: 'Let's have a bash even if it's only bacon and eggs.' It may be that your first view of the tiny galley with its small stove might easily make you support the first philosophy. However, any half-hearted attempt to use the galley by turning out just one long succession of frys could result in mass desertion by the crew. Yet some of the tastiest meals I've had have been in yachts where the cook has used just a little extra imagination and forethought.

But no one wants to spend too much time cooking on holiday, especially in a small boat, so a compromise is called for. Spend so much of your time eating ashore but allow for a few meals being cooked aboard. At some nightly mooring in a lonely bay you may have no choice. The lists of recipes I provide at the end of each area section have all been tried out successfully afloat and I think there will be some temptation to do your own thing once you have seen some of the delightful fresh foodstuffs in the southern European regions where flotilla yachting mostly takes place. The recipes given are all based on local cuisine and foodstuffs.

You will certainly need to prepare plenty of cold lunches and snacks for hungry 'sailors' whilst sailing between ports and the recipes include several suggestions for making these different using the good choice of salad ingredients found ashore. These need to be bought daily, if possible, as very few yachts boast a fridge — just a simple ice box or cold container with chemical packs that need freezing (local ice-cream shops will often do this for you).

An alternative to eating aboard or in a restaurant ashore is to have a barbecue on some isolated beach. It is fairly simple to make a temporary barbecue using driftwood, some suitable rocks and a piece of heavy wire netting (bought at a local hardware shop). Cooking in embers is another, even easier, way.

The type of meals cooked aboard will be limited, of course, by having just a couple of rings and a small oven, which is really more suitable for keeping food warm while waiting to be served. There is also a grill and this can prove one of the most useful parts of the stove as a goodly number of dishes can be prepared on it. See Chapter 4, Waterways Catering, for advice on grill cooking. I hardly need to warn about the danger of cooking while the yacht is underway as even in apparently calm seas your craft could suddenly lurch, spilling hot fat or liquids over you.

One warning you will certainly get from the hire company concerns the gas bottles that supply many yacht stoves. These are stowed in a purpose-built locker in the cockpit where there is less risk of any build-up of leaking gas. But an outside chance remains that the heavier-than-air gas might seep down into the bilges risking an explosion from a discarded cigarette end. For this reason you are advised not to let any time elapse between turning on the gas rings and lighting them. Have the lit match ready. You must also turn off the supply at the bottle when not in use and regularly pump the bilges dry. The gas smell is readily recognisable.

For what is in almost every sense a truly *al fresco* kind of holiday it seems a shame to add another piece of cautionary advice but I think most people will appreciate that dumping refuse overboard is frowned on very much in these anti-pollution days. Also, harbour masters do not like a port covered in jetsam. Rubbish bags are supplied aboard for you to leave refuse in an appropriate place ashore.

SHOPPING

Whether you intend to do much cooking aboard or not, one of the great joys on any yachting holiday around the Adriatic, Aegean or Mediterranean is wandering through the highly colourful displays of local produce in many of the ports visited. Apart from the appeal of a cornucopia of fruit, vegetables, cheeses, fish, eggs, rabbits and game, another attraction will be the cheap prices. But remember you have little storage space aboard, frozen or otherwise, so do not over-buy. Food does go off rapidly on yachts unless you stow some in a safe place on deck (not meat or fish which should be cooked as soon as possible in warm climates).

It is not so surprising, then, that I recommend buying

tinned as well as fresh goods. Canned meats such as cooked ham and chicken and packaged items such as instant soups and pastas will be more easily stowed and will not go off. You need not worry about the first day or two as the holiday company will have put some basic food items aboard. These will not amount to much, however, and I rather suspect that the operators prefer you to eat ashore so as to compensate for the smallness of the galley.

Having a reasonably good supply of stores on board is a wise precaution since you can often be well away from shops or somewhere that offers a limited choice, as on the smaller Greek and Yugoslav islands. There will be no problem finding most things in the larger towns you visit, although in Turkey, with its tougher economy, a lot of Western-style goods are absent. Several marinas have small shops selling essentials. You will also have no problem finding a good choice of drinks almost everywhere, particularly in Yugoslavia, where the aperitifs and liquors are very good. Wine is awash, though rather less so in Turkey.

Although you will have little space aboard, do take coffee, your favourite tea bags, breakfast cereal if possible, and some tins of meat if you can cram them in. These are either expensive or difficult to find in most of the countries visited.

EATING OUT

If your style of eating aboard is simple, you will soon find that your eating habits ashore will be just a degree or so grander. Many of the harbours you will visit have little more than small cafés with a limited menu. But in some of the bigger ports with fine restaurants you may opt for less pretentious places. Your style of dress, like your eating, gets distinctly casual after a few days afloat and dining out often becomes a lively party affair since you tend to stick with other crews from the same flotilla.

Although you are free to go your own way ashore almost everyone joins in the several happy-go-lucky meals that all companies arrange for their clients during the cruises — mostly barbecues on some isolated beach. For some you are expected to dress up, say as pirates. Drinks parties are also held on the 'mother ship'.

In the main areas where fleet sailing takes place, south-east Europe and near-Asia regions, most eating spots concentrate on local-type dishes and not on international cuisine. However, there is plenty that is tastily suitable, especially the fish meals that figure prominently, if nowadays, more expensively, in countries such as Greece and Yugoslavia. Turkey offers quite a rich and reasonably priced variety of dishes with the Dalmatian region close behind, whereas in the Greek ports you visit there is a somewhat repetitive selection.

In all the areas meal costs are reasonable, especially in Turkey and Yugoslavia. Snack bars and other fast-food places have become much more common in Yugoslavia and Greece although they are concentrated in the bigger towns and at most ports, being small, you will see very few. It's as well to remember that service in many of the cafés and restaurants is, like the local way of life, very easy going. One of the appeals in Greek and Turkish eating places is the way you are encouraged to choose your fish, meat, etc, before it is cooked by a visit to the kitchen or fish tank.

13

Yugoslavia

The thousands of islands along the Yugoslav coast form a magnificent long chain perfectly created for safe offshore yachting. Large, small, beautifully green or ruggedly bare they are also great places to visit with many charming, small harbours. Of course, you will be able to take in only a small selection of these islands in just a week or fortnight and you therefore have to select your route from one of several with bases spread along most of the Adriatic coast. Some of these routes also allow you to sail deep up fjord-like inlets in the mainland.

A big attraction of cruising almost anywhere off Yugoslavia is the wide variety of ports of call — including fine, old, well-preserved Roman cities like Split and Zadar; lovely small walled Venetian towns such as Korcula; modern package holiday resorts in Istria in the north; and many tiny deserted coves where you can swim in fine, clear water. Yet even when among the many islands you remain in clear sight of the coast, much of it sharply mountainous. Virtually everywhere you go offers a tasty selection of local food produce, wines and liqueurs. Eating ashore ranges from the substantial meat dishes beloved by the Yugoslavs to giant crayfish caught off many of the rockier islands.

Flotilla sailing has really taken off during the past few years with fleets based at key points for each stretch of the whole coastline. Starting in the north, in the region called Istria, you start your cruise from the interesting holiday resort of Rovinj or from the old city of Pula with its outstanding Roman remains. Of all the Yugoslav routes these stay closest to the tourist scene with several big package centres *en route*, although on one heading further south you do take in some attractive islands away from the main holiday scene. By comparison with the more rugged Dalmatian coast this region is gentler yet equally safe for yachting. There is a strong Italian influence here, too, with cities like Venice not that far away.

Further down the coast in the northern part of Dalmatia there are flotilla trips from the small harbours of Vodice and Jezera to a group of islands that are among the less populated and least visited. In central Dalmatia, from Split and another charming old port, Primosten, you can sail to the same group or head south to several of the most attractive and popular Yugoslav islands, Hvar, Brac and Korcula. Into southern Dalmatia, from the tiny harbour of Slano, you can also sail to the same places, plus the island nature reserve of Mljet. Or, using Slano, you can go down the lovely coastline to Dalmatia's star city Dubrovnik and still further south to the pleasant small resort of Cavtat. Permutations of most of the above routes are also possible.

When sailing from Pula and Split you are flown direct into their airports while for the others you can have an added road journey of an hour or two from airports at several points along the Yugoslav coast. In nearly all cases you use the same base for departure and return but it may be possible by special arrangement to leave your craft at a different terminal where the operator runs boats from both. A feature of cruising the Yugoslav coast not found anywhere else is the chain of duty free stores specially set up for the foreign yachtsmen. These are very useful for buying imported liquors and cigarettes, plus a few other types of goods, but drink and tobacco are relatively cheap in Yugoslavia anyway. A very favourable exchange rate to the pound sterling also makes the holiday cheaper.

FLOTILLA COMPANIES

With a couple of exceptions these are all specialist yacht firms. The others are tour operators offering sailing as part of a bigger holiday programme. They include:

Phoenix (a Yugoslav subsidiary), 16 Bonny St, London NW19PG (tel: 01485 5515)

Island Sailing, Northney Marina, Hayling Island, Hants PO110NH (tel: 0705 466331). This is linked with Seven Seas Sailing, at the same address but with a different phone number (0705 468922)

Sundown Yacht Charters, Rectory Lane, Woodmansterne, Surrey SM73PP (tel: 07375 51271)

Yacht Cruising Association, Old Stone House, Judges

Terrace, East Grinstead, Sussex RH191AQ (tel: 0342 311366)

Flotilla Sailing Holidays Ltd, 2 St John's Terrace, Harrow Rd, London W104RB (tel: 01969 5423)

Both Island Sailing and Seven Seas offer flotilla training courses at the Emsworth Sailing School, Hants, lasting 3-4 days.

Further details on Yugoslavia and its coastal attractions can be obtained from the Yugoslav National Tourist Office, 143 Regent St, London W1R4AR (tel: 01 734 5243).

CATERING IN YUGOSLAVIA

Of all the main regions described for flotilla sailing in this guide this is probably the one with the best and often most convenient possibilities for catering. On most routes you sail from or call at ports with quite good shops and open-air markets are found at a lot of places. The exceptions are some of the smaller, less populated islands, although even on these you can usually obtain fresh produce including both white fish and shellfish. The country has been going through some harder economic times of late so certain items common here may not always be available or can be a bit expensive. On the whole, thanks to a good rate of exchange for the pound sterling, you will find catering as cheap as almost anywhere in Europe.

SHOPPING

Many people believe that because Yugoslavia is a communist land everything in it is state owned. Not so. Private enterprise is flourishing and this includes many smaller shops with some larger ones run by independent 'enterprises' of a collective kind. If the competitive spirit is not so evident as in the West you will still find a fairly good range of groceries and as the locals love meat some quite good butchers with extensive displays. Yugoslav lamb and beef is worth buying. Canned cooked meats and sausages are also recommended, although much of the latter are very spicy. Pastas, too, are very common — thanks to past Italian colonisation. Most of the basic items you'll need can be found, including some excellent cheeses. However, there are some familiar goods you won't find like marmalade, cereals and most kinds of teas. Coffee is expensive, as are the few imported luxury foods.

The best places to shop are often in the open-air markets which, in bigger ports like Split, are often very extensive with massive displays of fresh vegetables, fruit, cheeses and meats. Frequently you can buy direct from farmers or local householders. Fishermen will also sell catches from their boats or at nearby markets. Real old-fashioned crusty loaves can be bought at the numerous local bakeries. Fresh milk is not always available so buy the powdered kind.

EATING OUT

One of the pleasures of dining out in Yugoslavia is the fascinating range of restaurants and cafés. You can eat in former convents and monasteries, modern hotels, Roman ruins or even in the backyard of a fisherman's home. Some spots are quite sophisticated while most are fairly simple, often in the open air. None are too expensive. There are also some wide variations in styles of cuisine. There is typical Serbo-Croat, heavy on meats, stews and spicier ingredients, and quite an array of Italian-inspired dishes from the days when Italians ruled parts of the coast. Intermixed are some recipes left over from Turkish domination and a sprinkling of Bosnian and Slovenian foods. And if none of these appeal you can always find the blander tourist-type meals in the package resorts.

Fish being the one thing that is both fairly common and less likely to be served differently to your normal taste, you will probably enjoy a lot of it. Among some local specialities

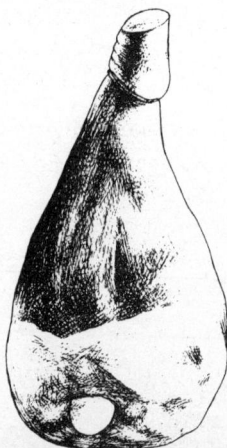

Presunto Ham

worth trying are *Brodet*, a tasty fish stew, and *Na Buzara*, crab boiled in seawater. Up some fjords you'll find oysters being bred and sold. On the rockier *Otoks* (islands) off the northern Dalmatian coast the local restaurants serve large crayfish (often mistakenly called lobster on the menu) as cheaply as you find almost anywhere. If you're lucky you might arrive somewhere when a local holiday is taking place and they are barbecuing a lamb or two. In these friendly places everyone is welcome. Do try the succulent Dalmatian ham that locals boast is finer than the better known Parma kind. Eaten with crusty local bread (or local farm cheeses) it makes a fine snack. It goes down far better with one of the many good (and strong) red wines each area produces.

HANDY SERBO-CROAT

It *is* called Serbo-Croat, the national language, not 'Yugoslav', although you will find several tongues used in different parts of the country. Italian and German are also understood by many along the coast and English is in more popular resort areas. There can be marked differences in dialect between Istria in the north and Dalmatia.

Common Phrases

Good morning	*Dobro Yutro*
Where is …?	*Gdyé yé …?*
Do you speak English?	*Govorite Engelski?*
Thank you	*Jvala*
Is it deep?	*Ye Doobokoh?*
What do you want?	*Shto Hochete?*
Be careful!	*Pazite!*
I want …	*Ya hochoo …*

Shopping

How much?	*Koliko?*
Beans	*Grah*
Beef	*Govedina*
Beer	*Pivo*
Bread	*Kruh*
Butter	*Maslats*
Cheese	*Sir ('seer')*
Chicken	*Piliché meso or Piletina*
Eggs	*Yaya*
Fish	*Riba*
Ice	*Led*

Lamb	*Yanyetina*
Meat	*Meso ('messo')*
Milk	*Mlyeko*
Olive oil	*Oolyé od masline*
Pork	*Svinyetina*
Wine	*Vino*

Eating Out

Where is a good (cheap) restaurant?	*Gde se nalasi dobin (jeftin) restoran?*
Where is a good restaurant for seafood?	*Gde se nalasi dobar restoran za morsku ribu?*
I should like a table near the window	*Voleo bih sto pored prozora*
I only want a snack	*Ja bih samo da prizalogajnem*
I like it underdone/medium/ well done	*Zeleo bih to nepeceno/ srednje peceno/dobro ispeceno*
I did not order this	*Ja ovo nisam narucio*
May I have the bill?	*Mogu li da platim?*

Ajvar	Salad with paprika mixed with aubergine
Alaska corbo	Soup made from freshwater fish
Bubrezi	Kidney
Cevapcici	Rolled meat on skewers with raw onions
Corba	Thick soup

Aubergines

Djuvec	Serbian meat stew sprinkled with cheese
Gibanica	Cheese and egg pie
Jaje	Egg
Jetra	Liver
Kapama	Spinach and leeks stewed with mutton
Kobasica	Sausage
Krompir	Potato
Kupus	Cabbage
Pastrmka	Trout
Pile	Chicken
Pirinac	Rice
Povrce	Vegetables
Predjelo	Hors d'oeuvres
Punjena paprika	Peppers stuffed with minced meat and rice
Raznjici	Similar to Turkish kebab
Recni rak	Crayfish
Riba	Fish
Sarma	Minced meat and rice in cabbage or vine leaves
Sir	Cheese
Sunka	Ham
Supa	Clear soup
Svinjetina	Pork
Teleca corba	Stewed veal, sausage, tomatoes, peppers cooked with cream and eggs
Deser	Dessert
Kolac	Cake
Sladoled	Ice-cream
Voce	Fruit

RECIPES

Yugoslav cuisine is one of the richest in Europe, reflecting centuries of living under so many invading powers from Austrian to Italian and Turkish. On the northern Istrian coast the Italian flavour is strongest and in the south of Dalmatia the Ottoman Empire has left its culinary mark. All along the Adriatic the Serbo-Croat style is strong. Many dishes are too spicy or rich for more northern tastes but the dishes presented below should be suitable both for your palate and for preparing in small galleys. Note that all the dishes can be served cold as well as hot and in the very warm Yugoslav summers the former might be preferable. They all go well with salads (see other sections for suggestions). My thanks for them are to Mrs Sonia Jakopovic, wife of the Managing Director of Phoenix, London, who arrange flotilla sailing.

Pepperonette

4 green peppers	1 lb (500 g) cooked or
4 tomatoes	smoked ham
1 aubergine	2 tablespoons olive or
1 large potato	cooking oil

Warm oil in pan; cut peppers in strips and fry for 3-4 minutes until soft. Add potato cut into small cubes and fry for 2-3 minutes more. Next add aubergine, peeled and cut in strips, along with chunks of tomato and ham. Cook whole for 2-3 minutes and season with a pinch of salt and black pepper at end.

Sausages, frankfurters and bacon can be substituted for the ham and bread can replace the potato.

Green and Red Peppers

Poor Man's Dish

8 oz (250 g) Gruyere (or	4 oz (125 g) butter
similar hard cheese)	1 lb (500 g) any type ham
6 eggs	Pinch of paprika and salt

Put meat, butter and salt in a pot and simmer for 2 minutes. Add 3 beaten eggs and cook until thickened. Add thinly sliced cheese, remaining 3 eggs and paprika and simmer for further few minutes.

Katchikaval's Pan

4 slices mature cheese
2 eggs
3 tablespoons flour

8oz (250g) breadcrumbs
3 tablespoons oil

Mix flour, beaten eggs, breadcrumbs and a few spoonfuls water. Coat sliced cheese in the mixture and fry in very hot oil for 5 minutes.

Dalmatian Risotto

2 tablespoons olive oil
1 large onion
1/2 lb (250g) Italian rice
Bacon rind or salt pork
Celery leaves

3oz (75ml) white wine
1 can of chicken stock
2oz (60g) grated Parmesan
 cheese

Heat oil in pan; sauté chopped onion until transparent; sprinkle rice in with onion and sauté for further 5 minutes. Add rind or pork and celery leaves followed by white wine. Cook for 5-10 minutes before adding enough chicken stock to cover. Reduce heat and boil for 15 minutes or until mixture is creamy. Sprinkle Parmesan on top.

Bosnian Pilav

4 tablespoons oil
1 medium onion
1-2 large tomatoes
1/2 lb (250g) rice
1 pint (1/2 litre) chicken
 stock or consommé

1 1/2 lbs (750g) currants
Knob of butter
Dill or rosemary
Parsley
Salt and pepper

Melt butter in pan and gently cook chopped onion. Add well-drained rice and cook for 5 minutes. Add currants and tomatoes and season with salt, pepper, dill or rosemary. Finally, add chicken stock or consommé and bring quickly to boil. Cook on for 15 minutes (first five minutes uncovered) until liquid is absorbed. Stir in chopped parsley at end.

14

Greece

Mention this country's name and most immediately think of the Aegean. In fact some people believe that the Aegean is the only Greek sea with cruising possibilities. But they ignore the very attractive, sometimes calmer, waters of the Ionian Sea off the country's west coast. Even the Aegean has to be divided into several distinct sailing areas, such as the Gulf of Salonika and the Saronic Gulf. And you can sail Turkish as well as Greek waters. Here I give details of the three flotilla sailing regions around Greece with the Turkish ones in a separate section.

Note: The Greek National Tourist Organisation, 195 Regent St, London W1R8DL (tel: 01 734 5997) supplies all information needed about holidaying in its country including details of tour and flotilla firms.

IONIAN

The trials that beset Odysseus trying to sail home to Ithaca, one of the Ionian islands, are hardly likely to befall you but you will get plenty of fun following over part of his wake at least. Almost certainly the storms that formed part of his hazards will be missing. Although it is called a 'sea' it is really that stretch of water that links the Adriatic with the Mediterranean and a good part of it can be seen more like an island-dotted lake — even an inland waterway in places. The passages between some islands and between islands and parts of the mainland are not much more than canal or river width at times. Islands like Levkas and Ithaca form what is almost an inland sea with the Peloponnese rounding off the illusion.

There are three main itineraries taking in the northern area as far as Corfu (really well detached from the rest) and

Paxos; the main central islands like Cephalonia, Ithaca and Levkas, and a more southerly route as far as Zante. In fact all these courses overlap and most operators allow you rather more freedom here to sail a bit where you will than in most waters — an indication of calmer seas. Totally independent yachting is also allowed here for the more experienced.

Whichever route you follow the unspoilt scenery and the local life and history are equally fascinating. The islands have so far avoided the mass package tourism of Corfu and although a good many Greeks take their holidays here in high season you will still find plenty of empty bays and uncrowded little harbours. What strikes visitors most, especially those used to the more barren Aegean islands, is the vivid greenery of these islands. They can also be more mountainous like Cephalonia while all are agriculturally productive. Fresh vegetables and fruit and certainly fresh water are more easily obtained than on many Greek islands elsewhere. Apart from a few, slightly larger harbours you might visit, shopping and eating out is fairly restricted to small stores and little cafés.

To get to most of the yacht bases you are flown to an airport in the western Peloponnese mainland and then by coach down the coast for two or three hours to one of three possible starting points. The most northerly is North Sivota (the North is important as you will see) on the mainland. Sometimes the company operating from here takes you on by ferry to join your yacht on the small island of Paxos. The other principal flotilla operators base their boats on what is called the island of Levkas but is really part of the mainland separated by a very narrow waterway. You board your craft at Sivota (no North) or Vasiliki, both small villages with a few tavernas. The holidays centred here and the islands immediately to the south are best for those who do not fancy too much open water as on the northern routes, including one that starts on Corfu (you fly direct there).

Flotilla Companies

The following are the main firms for the Ionian Sea currently operating there. From time to time other firms enter the scene and you should check with the Greek National Tourist Organisation (address above).

Falcon Sailing, 33 Notting Hill Gate, London W11 3JQ (tel: 01 727 0232)
Flotilla Sailing Holidays, 2 St John Terrace, Harrow Rd, London W10 4RB (tel: 01 969 5423)

Island Sailing, Northney Marina, Hayling Island, Hants, PO11 0NH (tel: 0705 466331)

Yacht Cruising Association, Old Stone House, Judges Terrace, Ship St, East Grinstead, Sussex RH10 1AQ (tel: 0342 311366).

Ionian Catering

Broadly speaking you can feed yourself aboard and ashore here very much as you can elsewhere in Greek waters. If there is a particular advantage it is the richer productiveness of the islands than is usually found in the Aegean. But that relates mainly to fresh fruit and vegetables and you will still need that good old standby — tinned meat: good butchers are few and far between. But fresh fish is reasonably plentiful. Tavernas and the harbour-side cafés (chips with everything here, too) feature prominently. For further details on catering, see the section Catering in Greece (pages 126-34).

AEGEAN

It may look reasonably small and cruise-handy on your school atlas but this sea is really far too big to attempt more than a corner of it for your holiday. You are also limited by the Aegean's not-so-well-publicised reputation for getting quite stormy in summer. Flotilla firms have wisely chosen certain areas where you can be surer of calmer 'wine dark seas'. But for bolder, more capable skippers they sometimes permit them to sail a bit further afield and more independently.

SARONIC GULF/PELOPONNESE/CYCLADES

Over the past 2,000 years and more quite a few sea battles have been fought in the deep gulf between that large area of Greece on which Athens stands and the Peloponnese. But nowadays it is a busy cruise water for yachts and small passenger ships. More sheltered in summer when some strong winds can disturb other parts of the Aegean, flotilla firms have chosen it for several of their programmes. These form an interesting mixture of island and mainland visits, small harbours and a few popular resorts, ancient ruins and modern tourism.

You are rarely far from land as you criss-cross between islands like Hydra, Aegina and Poros, all popular holiday places, and the mainland of the Peloponnese, where such famous ruins as Epidavros and Byzantine monasteries are more a feature. Most operators have chosen fairly similar routes that take in the adjoining Argolic Gulf and Hydra Gulf (both semi-landlocked and good for independent sailing). But some head a bit further north or south and one firm crosses the Saronic Gulf completely from a base on the southern edge of Athens. Some companies chose the small island of Poros at the Gulf's south-western point for their base. One company offers a one-way route between Korfos, on the Peloponnese opposite Aegina Island, and Astros in the Argolic Gulf, or vice versa.

All operators fly you into Athens airport but after that the transport to your base takes various routes and forms of transport, including coach and/or hydrofoil. Some of these transfers can take several hours with meal stop. The cost is included in the package price.

These cruises are recommended for the less experienced yachtsmen and women but anyone with greater ability may like to sail more independently deeper into the Aegean to the Cyclades — to well-known islands like Mykonos, Tinos and Delos, and a few less so such as Siros and Kithnos. More seaworthy but more difficult to handle yachts are provided.

Flotilla Companies

Island Sailing, Northney Marina, Hayling Island, Hants PO11 0NH (tel: 0705 46631)

Sundown Yacht Charters, Sundown House, Rectory Lane, Woodmansterne, Surrey SM7 3PP (tel: 07375 51271)

Yacht Cruising Association, Old Stone House, Judges Terrace, Ship St, East Grinstead, Sussex RH10 1AQ (tel: 0342 311366)

Seven Seas Sailing (same address as Island Sailing but phone no: 0705 468925)

Aegean Catering

With such a good choice of ports, including several busy tourist centres, catering is usually no problem. Some of the popular holiday islands have quite good supermarkets and a decent range of all types of shops. There is a respectable selection of fresh produce at most mainland harbours. A particularly good buy in the Peloponnese is olive oil, some of which is regarded as the most acid-free and among the best in the world. Considering the price in Britain I rate it a better buy to bring home than a so-called duty-free bottle of Scotch. It comes in cans as well as in bottles. For general advice on Greek catering, see pages 126-34.

SPORADES

These may sound more like the birthplace of Greek mytho-
logy but, in fact, they are to be rated more highly in yachting
history as a spawning ground of today's flotilla sailing. A
dozen years ago one of the very first ventures into fleet sailing began in these islands in the north-east of Greece. It is a
mark of the calm water pleasures for newcomers to yachting
(and the more practised) that they were first chosen. Since
then the three main islands around which you sail, Skiathos,
Skopelos and Skyros, along with a few mainland calls, have
become favourites with many conventional holidaymakers.

Quite a range of modern hotels have sprung up and you
will find plenty of fun in their resorts. But there are a few
unspoilt small islands in the group — Pelagos, Peristera,
Yioura and Skantzoura — almost totally deserted. Alonissos,
another larger island, offers a variety of scenes from the busy
port activity of its main town to the tranquillity of ancient
villages. What most distinguishes the Sporades from more
barren Aegean islands to the south (the group is further
north nearer the Gulf of Salonika) is the rich, wooded green-
ness. Farming and livestock is more common and traditional
ways seem better preserved — you could find some men on
some islands still wearing embroidered blouses and baggy
trousers.

Most routes stay within the Sporades, interweaving among
the islands, sometimes with calls at the same ones on both
outward and return legs, although never at the same port.
Not all cruises include Skyros, the place where Rupert
Brooke lies buried, for although it is one of the most charming islands it is some way detached from the main group.
One operator offers it as an optional extension for more
experienced skippers as the wind in July and August, the
strong Meltemi, can prove too boisterous for beginners.
Generally, the wind among the islands can often be fresh and
you need some confidence for sailing these waters.

To get to the Sporades you can fly direct from Britain into
Skiathos by charter flight (virtually all flotilla holidays include
charters), which is an indication of just how popular this
place has become. But one firm uses Athens airport and
coaches you over the protracted journey to Orei, a small
harbour on the north side of Evvia Island (almost part of the
mainland), from where you sail a broad sea channel to the
Sporades. It means seeing less of the group and more of
mainland harbours but you are often in calmer waters.

Flotilla Companies

Island Sailing, Northney Marina, Hayling Island, Hants
PO11 0NH (tel: 0705 466331)
Seven Seas Sailing (same address as above but phone no:
0705 468925)
Yacht Cruising Association, Old Stone House, Judges
Terrace, Ship St, East Grinstead, Sussex RH10 1AQ (tel:
0342 311366)

Sporades Catering

If you start your cruise at Skiathos you will have no problem
shopping. This bustling tourist resort has a wide range of
well-stocked stores, including supermarkets. And several
discos as well as a good array of eating places. The next two
islands, Skopelos and Alonissos, also have main ports with a
fair choice of shops and restaurants. But on several islands
there is nothing at all or just a single shop selling basics.
Anyone making an extension cruise to Skyros will find it a
useful restocking point. Fresh produce is easily available in
the more verdant Sporades and I recommend the tasty
plums, almonds and olives on Skopelos. Goats' milk is common if you fancy it. Tavernas will be your main eating spots
until returning to Skiathos to treat yourself at one of the choi-
cer restaurants there.

CATERING IN GREECE

The Greeks have always preferred to eat out so, with the
exception of larger towns, they do not worry too much about
providing such a wide range of shops as you find in many
other European countries. But they do, obviously, have many
cafés and restaurants that will tempt you to eat ashore rather
than aboard. On most of the flotilla routes, however, there
will be occasions in the smaller harbours when you must
cook something. Given that butcher's shops are not always
handy and that meat is often pricey, you are likely to fall back
on the good choice of fresh vegetables to form a substantial
part of main dishes. Cold collations will play a big part in
such a hot part of Europe.

Without a fridge you will rely heavily on tinned meats and
these are not always as common in Greece as in the UK.
Therefore it is wisest if you can take a few tins with you,
although the number has to be severely limited because of
their weight. Packaged instant foods are a handier substitute.
In some ports you can buy fresh caught fish like red mullet
but the Aegean is not as rich in seafood as it once was. The

Ionian is better. Flotilla companies place a few basic items aboard to help get you going but these are often just tea, coffee, sugar and the like. Take some of these items yourself as they can be expensive in Greece. Take milk in powdered or condensed form.

SHOPPING

Probably the best piece of advice to give strangers to Greece is to warn about food shop closing hours. As a general rule everything shuts in the afternoons and reopens in the evening but there can be a lot of variations in times and the days they apply. On Mondays, Wednesdays and Saturdays foodshops open from 8a.m. until 3p.m. (some do close sooner), whereas on Tuesdays, Thursdays and Fridays opening times are from 8a.m. to 2p.m. and from 5.30p.m. to 8.30p.m. (again there could be variations). Stick to shopping in the morning — it's safer.

Many Britons worry that meat sold in a hot country like Greece will carry health risks but many Greek butcher's shops are now very well refrigerated. Lamb is a best buy and usually the cheapest. There is also a wide choice of sausages (if spicy) but not so much cooked meats. Tinned sausages are best but the imported kind can be expensive. There is no problem getting a wide range of vegetables and the fruit is equally rich in variety. Always ensure you wash fruit since the dust it collects can be virulent, causing tummy upsets. Cheeses are usually made from goats' or ewes' milk and are very tangy and dry. Yoghurt is plentiful too. Milk is usually the sterilised kind and with no proper fridge aboard you may prefer using milk powder. Do not forget the mineral water: tap water in Greece can either be over-chlorinated or risky. Cheap, reasonable wine is easy to find and there is always *ouzo* and local brandy. The *retsina* may not be to your taste but is very refreshing.

One local foodstuff not to be missed is the most basic — bread. In many of the small ports visited you will find it being baked in ancient ovens in the same way it has been done for centuries. The same ovens are often used by locals for cooking their Sunday dinners. Beautifully crusty it is a darn sight more healthy and satisfying than our steam-baked spongy loaves.

EATING OUT

There are purists who argue that there is no such thing as a Greek cuisine — that it is all inherited from the Turkish conquerors of old. Even if the theory is correct do not mention it to the Greeks or you might get your *dolmadhes* thrown rather than on a plate. For the same reason it is always better to ask for Greek coffee and not 'Turkish', even if it does look exactly the same. The fact is that in many Greek hotels and popular tourist resorts the food is a bland international fare and for the 'Greek' kind you need to hunt out certain restaurants. The tavernas and small cafés, of course, serve local dishes, although the variety is not great and nearly always the same wherever you go. Always check the price first as some restaurants tend to hide the cost.

A typical menu will usually include: hors d'oeuvres, *kalamaris* (squid), whitebait, garlic dip, *taramasalata* (cod roe salad), olives, stuffed tomatoes, peppers and aubergines, *dolmadhes* (stuffed cabbage or vine leaves) and various fish roes in different sauces or dressings. Main courses can include a choice of pastas; rice dishes; fish (usually expensive); lamb, veal, beef (also costly); various sausages, pork, meat balls and kebabs — not forgetting the inevitable chicken. *Moussaka* is a standard item. Very sweet pastries, *crème caramel* and fruit salads form many 'sweet' offerings (for a country with so much fresh fruit the canned kind appears remarkably often). These menus may not look much different to our own but the flavour can be quite different and the Greeks liberally use olive oil with most things.

HANDY GREEK

English is spoken more commonly in Greece these days but you will visit many more isolated places where few, if any, understand it. Since the written language is in characters so different to the Latin kind you have to rely heavily on just the spoken word. A grasp of classical Greek taught at school might help but modern Greek used by the public at large has much that is different. Fortunately you will find that menus in most restaurants and cafés have (often quite hilarious) English translations.

Common Phrases

Where is/are ...?   *Pou ine ...?*
How far is it to ...?   *Posso apehi ...?*
Have you ...?   *Ehete ...?*

May I have …?	*boro na eho …?*
Do you speak English?	*Milate Anglika?*
Good morning/Good day	*Kalimera sas*
How much is it?	*Posso ine?*

Shopping

Where is the market?	*Pou ine i aghora?*
… baker?	… *psomas?*
… butcher?	… *hasapis?*
… dairy?	… *ghalaktopolion?*
… grocer?	… *bakalis?*
Where can I buy …?	*Pou boro n'aghorasso …?*

Apple	*milo*
Bread	*psomi*
Cheese	*tiri*
Chicken	*kotopoulo*
Coffee	*kafes*
Egg	*avgho*
Fig	*siko*
Fish	*psari*
Fruit juice	*himos frouton*
Grapes	*stafili*
Honey	*meli*
Ice cream	*paghoto*
Jam	*marmeladha*
Lettuce	*marouli*
Mineral water	*metaliko nero*
Oil	*ladhi*
Olive	*elia*
Orange	*portokali*
Pear	*ahladhi*
Pepper	*piperi*
Plum	*dhamaskino*
Rice	*rizi*
Roll (bread)	*psomaki*
Salt	*alati*
Sauce	*saltsa*
Sausage	*loukaniko*
Strawberry	*fraoula*
Sugar	*sahari*
Tea	*tsai*
Tomato	*domata*
Vegetables	*lahanika*
Vinegar	*xidhi*

Watermelon	*karpouzi*
Wine	*krassi*

Eating Out

Can you suggest a good cheap restaurant?	*Borite na mou sistissete ena kalo fthino estiatorio?*
Is there a table free on the terrace?	*Iparhi kanena elefthero trapezi stin taratsa?*
Do you serve snacks?	*Ehete mezedhes?*
Can you tell me what this is?	*Ti ine afto?*
Is there a set menu?	*Ine to table d'hote?*
This isn't what I ordered	*Dhen parangila afto/thelo*
The bill, please	*Parakalo to loghariasmo*

Soupes	Soups
Kotossoupa	Chicken soup
Psarossoupa	Fish soup
Soupa lahanikon	Vegetable soup
Orektika ke prota	Hors d'oeuvres
Kalamarakia	Fried baby squid
Maridhes	Whitebait
Taramasalata	Cod roe salad
Thalassina	Shellfish
Anginares	Artichokes
Arni	Lamb
Arnissies brizoles	Lamb chops
Astakos	Lobster
Avgha	Eggs
Avgha tighanitamatia	Fried eggs
Barbouni	Red mullet
Bizelia	Peas
Brizola	Chop
Dolmadhes	Stuffed cabbage leave or vine leaves

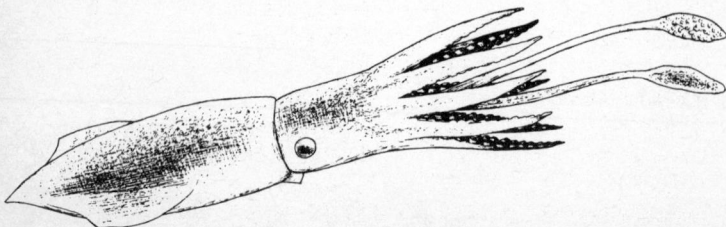

Squid

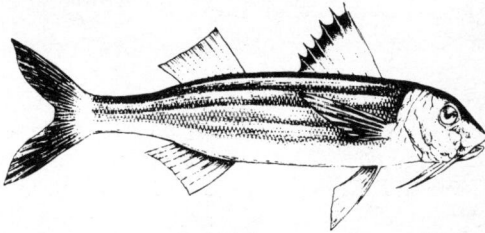

Red Mullet

Feta	White cheese, made from lamb or goat's milk
Fileto skharas	Grilled steak
Freska fassolakia	Green beans
Ghemistes domates	Stuffed tomato
Ghemistes piperies	Stuffed peppers
Ghemistes melidzanes	Stuffed aubergines
Ghlossa	Sole
Hirines brizoles	Pork chops
Kasseri	Cheddar-like cheese made from lamb's milk
Kefalotiri	Like Parmesan cheese
Keftedhes	Meat balls
Kotopoulo	Chicken
Kounoupidhi	Cauliflower
Kreas	Meat
Kremidhi	Onion
Lahano	Cabbage
Loukanika	Sausages
Manitaria	Mushrooms
Manouri	Creamy
Melidzanes	Aubergine
Mosharissies brizoles	Veal chops
Nefra	Kidneys
Pahanika ke soupes	Vegetables and Salads
Pilafi	Rice pilaf
Podhi kotas	Chicken leg
Psari	Fish
Psari skharas	Grilled fish
Psito hirinou	Roast pork
Psito psari	Baked fish
Sikoti	Liver
Sinaghridha	Red snapper
Souvlakia	Kebab
Spanaki	Spinach

Sparagia	Asparagus
Stithos kotas	Chicken breast
Tighanita psaria	Fried fish
Tyria	Cheese
Vrasta avgha	Boiled eggs
Xifios	Swordfish
Baklava	Crispy pastry with nuts and honey
Ghiaourti	Yoghurt
Ghliki smata	Desserts
Krema	Pudding
Pastes	Pastry
Paghoto	Ice cream

RECIPES

Most Greek dishes are reasonably simple to prepare even in yacht galleys, especially those using fresh vegetables and cheese mixed with meats. There is, of course, a close resemblance to Turkish cuisine and the recipes given at the end of the Turkish section can also apply here and vice versa.

Greek Salad

Cos lettuce cut into pieces	*Kalamata in the*
Strips of green pepper	*Peloponnese if possible)*
3 or 4 quartered tomatoes	*¼lb (125g) of Feta cheese*
Onion rings	*cut into cubes*
1 dozen black olives (from	

Toss whole in dressing of olive oil and lemon juice with a pinch of salt and black pepper added. You can sprinkle chopped fennel or dill over it and add a few gherkins if you like.

Olives

Lamb Cooked with Cheese

Leg of lamb   Salt and pepper
Feta cheese (or Kefalotiri)   Vine leaves

Season slices of leg of lamb with salt and pepper. Wrap tightly with slice of Feta or Kefalotiri cheese in oiled aluminium foil and cook gently for an hour until tender. It tastes better if you also line the foil with vine leaves that have been poached in water for just a minute. This dish can be eaten cold.

Spanakopitta

2 sheets Phylo dough $\frac{1}{2}$lb (250g) Feta cheese
2lb (1kg) fresh spinach   Pepper
3-4 tablespoons olive oil   Grated nutmeg
1 large chopped onion

This recipe uses the Phylo dough made of flour and water and rolled wafer thin that you can buy almost everywhere in Greece and is sold in packets (it needs to be well covered as it dries out quickly). Chop the spinach coarsely after removing thicker stems. Fry onion in the oil until golden. Add spinach stirring until tender. Add cheese and seasonings. Place two sheets of Phylo together after brushing each with melted butter. Place a good line of filling along a longer edge and roll up folding ends in as you go. Place rolls on greased baking tray (or shallow dish if tray not aboard) and place in pre-heated oven at 180°C for around $\frac{3}{4}$ hour until crisp.

Taramasalata

Grey mullet roe   White bread
Lemon juice   Grated small onion
Olive oil

Make a paste of grey mullet roe (smoked cod and other roes will do) by pounding well with lemon juice, liberal olive oil and white bread that has been soaked in water. Paste should have consistency of mayonnaise. A finely grated small onion can also be included. Serve with thin toast (or *pitta* bread) and black olives. Best eaten at once aboard and is normally kept cool in the fridge if prepared sometime beforehand.

Tomatoes

Pitta Picnic

Pitta bread
Tuna fish
Olives

Sliced tomatoes
Cucumber

The flat, hollow *pitta* bread which is common in the Middle East (and in Britain in some places) is also sold everywhere in Greece. It is admirable for on-board snacks and for picnics ashore. But it is better warm than cold. Its attraction is that you can fill it with almost anything. A simple way of using it is to make a sandwich using tuna, olives, slices of tomato and cucumber sprinkled with a dressing. Some Greeks fill them with seafood, melted cheese and meats to make an Italian-style stuffed pizza. One way of preparing tasty *pitta* is to wrap them (filled) in foil and heat in moderate oven.

15

Turkey

It has taken a long time for British tourists do discover the seductive charms of that south-west corner of Turkey where the Aegean meets the Mediterranean. For this sharply indented coastline of deep inlets and long peninsulas is a first-class region for flotilla sailing or the independent kind. Even now numbers are not that great and an unusually large proportion of tourists spend their holidays there afloat. The number of yacht companies operating there is growing all the time, while existing fleets get ever larger.

The fact that one can now fly direct by charter aircraft from Britain right into the region has helped open it up and its popularity for yachtsmen and women is bound to increase because of the coast's several advantages. These include the opportunity to cruise half a dozen different routes suitable for all standards; the good choice of nearly as many bases; the unusual fascination of both scenery and many lovely old towns along with an ancient way of life; and, not least, cheap shopping and eating out.

There are few more attractive harbours around the eastern Mediterranean/Aegean than Marmaris and Bodrum, two marvelously picturesque old towns from which flotilla cruises operate. Marmaris is also a big international yacht base nowadays. Another pretty place you sail from is Fethiye but almost everywhere you go there are charming ports, many little changed from past centuries. In one of the many pleasantly simple eating places you might find the waiters fishing for your lunch. A few steps from your yacht could be a typical Turkish bazaar or market overflowing with tasty fresh produce.

The route you choose depends very much on your ability for there are a few with longer, open stretches where the wind blows strong. Autumn is regarded as the calmest holiday period. In most cases your base is within an hour or two of the airport at Dalaman, midway between Marmaris and Fethiye. Bodrum is further away.

The area most companies have selected for gentler, safer cruising is between Marmaris and Fethiye with a route taking you into bays large and small and around a number of pleasant islands. There is also another itinerary with a good amount of sheltered water heading more westerly from Marmaris into the Dorian Gulf with its many nooks and crannies and, like several other parts of the coast, some really interesting old Greek and Roman remains to be visited. One company based on Bodrum includes the Dorian (sometimes called Symi) Gulf along with the very big Gulf of Gokova, another reasonably wind-shielded water where you can call at several tiny ports almost cut off from the rest of Turkey by mountains.

The coast east of Fethiye is usually kept to more experienced skippers as there is a long expanse of open sea all the way to Kekova, although you do call in at some interesting harbours *en route*. Among some permutations of the above routes more able skippers can also sail from Kas near Kekova across to Datca in the Dorian Gulf, starting or ending their cruise at either port. An extension from the latter area to Bodrum is also possible on voyages from Marmaris.

FLOTILLA COMPANIES

The following are companies currently operating in the region described but other yacht firms could well be starting up out there so check with the Turkish Tourist Office, 170 Piccadilly, London W1V 9DD (tel: 01 738 8681).

Falcon Sailing, 33 Notting Hill Gate, London W11 3JQ (tel: 01 727 0232)
Island Sailing, Northney Marina, Hayling Island, Hants PO11 0NH (tel: 0705 466331)
Sundown Yacht Charters, Rectory Lane, Woodmansterne, Surrey SM7 3PP (tel: 07375 51271)
Yacht Cruising Association, Old Stone House, Judges Terrace, East Grinstead, Sussex RH19 1AQ (tel: 0342 311366)

CATERING IN TURKEY

There was a time not long ago when any guide to the remoter parts of Turkey would have carried a warning about where and what you ate. Eating places and the manner in which some foodstuffs were sold were not exactly to our more sophisticated Western tastes. But one of the benefits of tourism is that it has done much to improve local catering. Admittedly it has made meals blander in some countries but in Turkey they have succeeded in preserving their inimitable cuisine while improving its hygiene and presentation. Just as well, for Turkish dishes are among the most internationally outstanding.

In the region where flotilla sailing takes place you are fortunate that as well as many local eating spots like fishermen's diners there are quite a good number of special tourist restaurants. A choice of food shops has also sprung up, although their range of goods can be much more limited than here. But you do have the advantage of good markets at most reasonably-sized ports and colourfully tempting places these are with a fine choice of fresh fruit and vegetables. Fresh fish is also a big attraction on this coast, very easily bought direct or eaten in several tempting ways at numerous seafood restaurants.

Octopus

My caution given for other yachting regions about taking certain basic items with you definitely applies here. You would imagine, for instance, there would be no problem getting coffee in the home land of Turkish coffee, but because of severe economic restrictions it is not only expensive but sometimes difficult to buy in shops. But don't worry about tea: the kind produced in Turkey can be excellent. If you can find room, take some tinned meats and packaged foods of the easy-to-prepare kind. Some operators place simple basics aboard.

It is one coast where you may never need to eat aboard and you could not be criticised for dining ashore when presented with such a good choice of cafés and restaurants. However, I offer some suggestions for those who like to go it alone or experiment with Turkish-style catering.

SHOPPING

Supermarkets have still to become a main feature of smaller Turkish towns where the concentration, thankfully, is still on specialist shops. You do, however, find some quite modern grocers with a choice of foodstuffs from the canned to frozen kind. But fresh food is preferred and you may find it difficult getting some of the ready-cooked and preserved items that better suit yacht catering. There is no problem, though, in buying meat and fowl, such as lamb in all its forms (including that roasted on a spit) and ready-cooked chicken as well as the fresh type. Remember this is a Muslim country where pork and hams are usually unknown.

Take full advantage of the traditional ways of shopping and head straight for the quaint local bakeries, where you can buy the most satisfying bread you've ever eaten, and the often-enclosed produce markets. Fish is easily found and not only in special markets but straight from your boats. This is a fairly mountainous coast so it is not always possible to find farms where fresh fruit, vegetables and eggs can be bought but some householders will sell you the odd item (or even give it free). Rely on powdered or condensed milk but do try the yoghourt since this is its birthplace. It's not what your milkman delivers as it is totally natural.

You will find that in spite of living in Asia many Turks have a more Western attitude than some nearby Europeans. This is reflected in such things as shop opening times: usually 9 a.m. to 1 p.m. and 2 p.m. to 7 p.m. on all the days of the week except Sunday when they are totally closed. But there can be variations according to regional laws.

EATING OUT

There is a common saying of seasoned travellers that the more modern and stylised a restaurant looks on the outside the poorer the food is inside. If that is true then many Turkish eating places look guaranteed to provide excellent cuisine! However, this is not entirely indicative of all and the rule is not to be deterred by appearances and choose certain menu items that are generally always worth eating. Lamb, of course, is one of them and it comes in more ways than the popular kind of spit roasting and kebabs. Incidentally, the latter is often just a straightforward affair of nothing but lamb on skewers.

I have known foreigners raise some waiters' eyebrows by commenting that much of the food 'looks Greek'. In fact it's the Greeks who inherited Turkish cuisine. In Turkey you will find *dolmas* (stuffed aubergines, vine leaves and peppers), the pilav rice dishes and the meat and cheese ones in flaky pastry while *baklava* and other honey sweets feature prominently. If there is one form of food you will definitely try along the coast it will be the several kinds of freshly-caught fish (sometimes right off the restaurant).

The Turks had snack bars and other instant food places long before we caught the habit, although you may not fancy eating from some of the simple stalls, especially in fly-ridden high summer. But try some of the fried vegetable tit-bits and the fresh baked breads of the *pitta* kind. Wash any fruit you buy as the dust is quite potent. Of course you will want to drink Turkish coffee and every village has its *kahve* (coffee house) — usually packed with males, many playing backgammon. You may even find a few smoking the *nargile* or hubble-bubble pipes.

I have not found many countries as cheap for dining out as Turkey, be it food or drink. There is a selection of wines, not all good, and liquor is not as common in variety as most countries. *Raki* — the local hooch — is an acquired taste.

HANDY TURKISH

English has become more commonly understood in recent years, not only because of tourism but because so many Turks have found work in the West before returning home. But you will visit some isolated harbours where no one at all might speak English. The complexities of Turkish really make it essential you take a language guide. The following is just a brief, handy selection.

Common phrases

Where is/are ...?	*Nerededkir ...?*
Is it far?	*Uzak mi?*
Have you ...?	*Var mi ...?*
I want ...?	*Istiyorum ...?*
Do you speak English?	*Ingilizce bilir misiniz?*
Where can I cash travellers' cheques?	*Nerede seyahat ceki bozabilirim?*
Thank you	*Teshekur-ederim*
Yes/No	*Evet/Yok (or Hayir)*

Shopping

Where is the market?	*Pazar veri nerede?*
... baker?	*... firinci/ekmekci?*
... butcher?	*... kasap?*
... grocer?	*... bakkal?*
... dairy?	*... sutcu dukkani?*
How much is it?	*Bu ne kadar?*
Give me a kilo/half a kilo ...	*Luften bir kilo/yarum kilo*

Apple	*elma*
Banana	*muz*
Bread	*ekmek*
Beef	*sigir eti*
Cheese	*peynir*
Coffee	*kahve*
Egg	*yumurta*
Fig	*incir*
Fish	*balik*
Fruit juice	*meyve suyu*
Grapes	*uzum*
Ice cream	*dondurma*
Lamb	*kuzu*
Melon	*kavun*

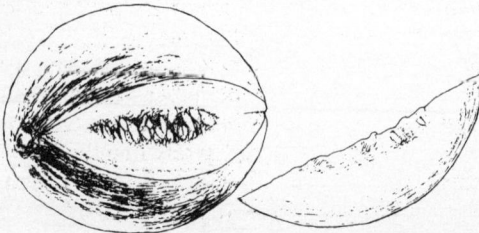

Melon

Milk	*sut*
Mineral water	*maden suyu*
Oil	*yag*
Olive	*zeytin*
Orange	*portokal*
Peach	*seftali*
Pear	*armut*
Pepper	*biber*
Plum	*erik*
Rolls (bread)	*ufak somun*
Salt	*tuz*
Soup	*corba*
Strawberry	*cilek*
Sugar	*seker*
Tea	*cay (chai)*
Veal	*dana eti*
Vinegar	*sirke*
Watermelon	*karpuz*
Wine	*sarap*

Eating Out

Can you suggest a good/cheap restaurant?	*Iyi bir restoran/ucuz bir restoran tavsiye edebilir misiniz?*
Do you serve snacks?	*Ufak porsiyon yemek servisi yapar misiniz?*
I'd like ...	*Istiyorum ...*
This isn't what I ordered, I want ...	*Siparis ettigim bu degildir, isterim ...*
The bill, please	*Hesabi getirin, lutfen*

For more common translations of certain main foods see under Shopping. The following are dishes often found in Turkish restaurants:

Arnavut cigeri	Spiced fried liver with onion
Bonfile	Fillet steak grill
Bulgur pilav	Cracked wheat pilaf
Cacik	Cucumber and yoghourt salad
Cerkes tavugu	Cold chicken in walnut purée
Cig kofte	Spicy raw meatballs
Coban salatasi	Tomato, pepper, cucumber and onion salad
Doner kebap	Lamb grilled on revolving spit
Dugun corbasi	Meat with egg yolks

141

Ic pilav	Rice with nuts, currants and onions
Imam bayildi	Aubergine with tomatoes and onions
Patlican kizartmasi	Fried aubergine with yoghurt
Patlican salatasi	Puréed aubergine salad
Pirzola	Lamb chops
Sade pilav	Plain rice pilaf
Sigara boregi	Fried filo pastry with cheese
Sis kebap	Grilled lamb on skewers
Sis kofte	Grilled meatballs
Talas boregi	Puff pastry with meat
Tarama	Fish roe salad
Yaprak dolmasi	Stuffed vine leaves
Yayla corbasi	Yoghourt soup
Baklava	Flaky pastry with nuts and syrup
Tel kadayif	Shredded wheat with nuts and syrup

RECIPES

The country's dishes would not need to be appetising to have an inimitable appeal. Many of their names are distinctly romantic (or odd!) Not many men could refuse 'Lady's Thighs' — or 'Lady's Navel' for that matter. But you might hesitate when confronted by 'The Priest Fainted'. The simplicity of preparing and cooking the recipes, however, is more important to yacht chefs. Fortunately, many Turkish dishes involve little more than your two-ring stove and small oven. Some are useful for picnics and barbecues. Many hot dishes are served on rice and a main vegetable is often aubergine. Yoghourt is a common ingredient.

Almonds

Cacik (Cucumber and Yoghourt)

1½lb (750g) yoghourt
2 small cucumbers
⅓ small cup olive oil

Few sprigs dill
Crushed garlic clove

Put yoghourt in salad bowl and beat well. Cut peeled cucumbers into small, thin pieces and place in yoghourt. Add most of oil, and the garlic and salt. Mix well. Apportion mixture in four bowls, garnish with dill and gently pour remaining oil in a fine thread over top.

Imam Bayildi (The Priest Fainted)

5 medium aubergines
5 medium onions
1½ cups water
¾ glass olive oil (less if preferred)

3 cloves garlic
1 medium tomato
Chopped parsley
Salt to taste

Remove aubergine stems, peel and cut into long narrow strips. Cook in olive oil on both sides. Cut onion into rings and garlic into small pieces and brown together in frying pan, adding chopped parsley. Put remaining aubergines, sliced in halves, into baking dish, removing seeds beforehand. Put onion, garlic and parsley mix into cavities. Garnish each half with a tomato ring. Pour remaining oil in bottom of dish and cook in warm (not hot) oven for 20-30 minutes. Serve cold.

Ic Pilav (Rice Pilau)

2½ cups rice
8-10 tablespoons margarine
1 medium tomato
1 desertspoon sugar
1 spoonful pine nuts (or similar)
1 sprig dill
Black pepper

Mixed spices
Cinnamon
Salt
3 cups water (or stock)
1 medium onion
½ lambs' liver (or chickens')
1 spoonful currants

Chop liver finely (after removing skin). Heat 2 tbspns margarine in pan and fry liver in it. Put remaining margarine in a pan and fry nuts and onions until latter are transparent. Add the rice after washing it well and fry for 10 minutes. Add black pepper, cinnamon, spice, water (or stock), currants, salt, sugar and chopped tomato. Cover with lid. Boil until rice has absorbed water and then cook gently. When rice is ready add fried liver and its fat. Mix in finely chopped dill and cook on for few minutes.

Weights and Measures

The following tables are approximate and simplified for easy conversion.

SOLID

Ounces	Grams
1/2	15
1	30
2	60
2 1/2	75
3	90
3 1/2	100
4	120
5	150
6	180
7	210
8	250
9	280
10	300
11	330
12	360
1 lb	500
2 lb	1 kg
3 lb	1 1/2 kg

LIQUID

British Imperial	Metric
1 fl oz	25 ml
2 fl oz	50 ml
3 fl oz	75 ml
4 fl oz	100 ml
5 fl oz	125 ml
1/2 pt	1/4 litre
1 pt	1/2 litre
1 1/4 pt	3/4 litre
1 3/4 pt	1 litre

American	Metric
1 fl oz	30 ml
2 fl oz	60 ml
3 fl oz	90 ml
4 fl oz	120 ml
5 fl oz	150 ml
1/2 pt	1/4 litre
1 pt	1/2 litre
1 1/2 pts	3/4 litre
2 pts	1 litre

OVEN TEMPERATURES

	Centigrade	Gas	Fahrenheit
Very cool	130°C	½	250°F
	140°C	1	275°F
Cool	150°C	2	300°F
Warm	170°C	3	325°F
Moderate	180°C	4	350°F
Fairly hot	190°C	5	375°F
	200°C	6	400°F
Hot	220°C	7	425°F
Very hot	230°C	8	450°F
	240°C	9	475°F
	250°C	10	500°F

MEASUREMENTS

0.4 in	1 cm
0.8 in	2 cm
1.2 in	3 cm
1.6 in	4 cm
2 ins	5 cm
2.4 ins	6 cm
2.8 ins	7 cm
3 ins	8 cm
3.5 ins	9 cm

Index

INLAND WATERWAYS

FLOTILLA SAILING

INDEX

Safety measures 99,
100-1, 104, 108
Sewage/anti-pollution
100, 108
Shopping 108; see also
in regional sections
Shoregoing 106
Snorkelling 101
Swimming 104

Tourist organisations
see listed in country
sections

Washing 104

Yachts
Description of
flotilla craft 99
Engines 99
Experience needed 97
Galleys 99
Handling 99, 103
Instruction 97, 113
Layout/fittings 99,
102
Safety 99

149